FAR BETTER
COACHING

INVESTING

WITH A

FULL DECK

What Las Vegas Taught Me
About Managing Money

JOE CHRISTIAN

FAR BETTER
C O A C H I N G

This publication contains the opinions and ideas of its author. It is sold with the understanding that neither the author nor the publisher is engaged in rendering legal, tax, investment, insurance, financial, accounting, or other professional advice or services. If the reader requires such advice or services, a competent professional should be consulted. Relevant laws vary from state to state. The strategies outlined in this book may not be suitable for every individual and are not guaranteed or warranted to produce any particular results.

No warranty is made with respect to the accuracy or completeness of the information contained herein, and both the author and publisher specifically disclaim any responsibility for any liability, loss or risk, personal or otherwise, which is incurred as a consequence, directly or indirectly, of the use and application of the contents of this book.

ISBN: 978-1-7357818-0-8
e-ISBN: 978-1-7357818-1-5

Book design by Grzegorz Japoł.

In Investing with a Full Deck, Joe demonstrates an insightful understanding of the human psyche that unblurs the lines between the world of money management and the poker table. There are the investor and the gambler, the patient and the anxious, the stoic and the emotional—all distinguishing traits that separate the winners from the losers. I have hired successful poker players as money managers, and I have witnessed many retired hedge fund managers go on to become successful poker players. There is often genius in simplicity, and this book is just that. The reader is furnished with the step-by-step guidance necessary to win the game of achieving financial independence. A fascinating read.

—**Louis Bacon**,
founder, chairman, and principal investment manager, Moore Capital, a multibillion-dollar hedge fund

Humorous and instructive. Thank you for connecting the dots.

—**Michael Bologna**,
partner, NovaQuest Capital Management

> *Who knew there could be a fascinating, engaging, and even gripping book about investing? Well, this is it. And it's a book about life. Short, punchy chapters will entertain you and give you plenty of guidance about the most important issues for prosperity and happiness. It's full of great stories and memorable quotes. I wish I had read this as a young man. Enjoy!*
>
> —**Tom Morris**,
> best-selling author of *If Aristotle Ran General Motors*, *The Art of Achievement*, *Plato's Lemonade Stand*, and *The Oasis Within*, among many other books

> *Joe has written a fun, easy-to-read financial guide to life. I wish it had been required reading in college.*
>
> —**Munroe Cobey**,
> retired partner, Tudor Investment Corporation

> *Joe Christian has demonstrated a great talent for storytelling. Making complex things simpler to understand cannot be underestimated when it comes to making significant changes. Changes for the better! Lots of fabulous nuggets of wisdom here!*
>
> —**Joe Cross**,
> filmmaker, *Fat, Sick, and Nearly Dead*

Insightful and provocative. With a unique gift for telling a good story, Joe engages the reader in such a way that the mystique of investing becomes a little less murky. The perfect guide to becoming a do-it-yourself investor.

—**Mike Battistelli**,
founder and owner, Alert Marketing Inc.

Joe Christian has written a great financial book that will blow your mind. He has created a holistic plan to help you address any preconceived views you may have around money and expand those to guide you to achieve your wildest dreams. If you're looking to get out of debt and gain financial freedom, this book is for you.

—**Amanda Chay**,
founder, Wonderment Ltd.

To my three amazing daughters,

Emily, Hanna, and Grace.

Your love and support

fuel my passion more than you will ever know.

There is no greater wealth

than having you in my life.

THE DECK

MINDSET

KNOWLEDGE

EXECUTION

INTRODUCTION

> ❝ *The only true wisdom is in knowing you know nothing.*
>
> —Socrates

My first visit to Las Vegas was during the summer of 1978. Two incompletes shy of my Duke diploma, I was sick and tired of school and ready for an adventure. I all but coerced a fraternity brother to join me on this expedition, and we took off in my van, loaded with all the required supplies, and headed for the West Coast. I'm not sure he's ever forgiven me.

As we pulled into Las Vegas, I recall seeing a thermometer that read 115 degrees shortly before my van's water pump decided to stop working. After having it replaced for around one hundred dollars—a lot of money in those days—I took my first stab at financial planning. I came up with the brilliant idea to recoup that unforeseen expense at the blackjack table. After all, I was quite the card player, possessing exceptional mathematical skills and a unique "sixth sense" that allowed me to predict what cards were coming. My confidence level was high.

But my so-called skills were of little help. The truth is, I had no idea what I was doing. The result? I lost the monetary equivalent of three water pumps and promptly left town with my tail between my legs and a much thinner bankroll.

After that Vegas excursion, my confidence in my blackjack skills waned, and I came to realize that if I was going to risk my money at a blackjack table, it might be a good idea to take the time necessary to learn how to play the game correctly. I soon discovered and now know that there is a correct play—be it hit, stand, split, double down, surrender, or fold—for every scenario. Making decisions based on intuition is foolhardy. However, what is known as *basic strategy*—derived from running millions of computer simulations—is readily available for you to learn, should you take the time to look. Numbers don't lie. This strategy can be mastered in a few hours, regardless of your aptitude, and it should dictate your decisions at the table. If you follow this strategy, you reduce the house edge to less than 1 percent.

With my newly acquired blackjack expertise, I went back to Vegas a few years later and carefully observed how others at the table were playing their hands. It didn't take me long to discern who knew how to play and who did not. I still cringe when watching players betting hundreds of dollars a hand while having no clue how to play the game.

It only makes sense for a blackjack player to invest a few hours of their time in becoming knowledgeable and preparing for the game before throwing their money away. But the reality is that few do. Careless blackjack players might as well be playing the slot machines. I, for one, have no interest in contributing my hard-earned dollars to an already-thriving business. Neither should you.

I rarely play blackjack these days because, even with that small house edge, it is a losing game over the long haul. No longer do I enjoy playing any games in which I find myself at a disadvantage. Better to have the edge and exploit it.

I may have overestimated my natural ability to play blackjack, but there's no underestimating my ability to sell. From an early age, I relied on my sales ability to put money in my pocket. If there was money to be made selling anything, I sold it. My gift of gab served me well. It was only fitting that I ended up in the financial services arena. I wanted to make a lot of money, and at the time, becoming a stockbroker provided the means to my end.

Armed with a degree in economics from Duke University (yes, I made up those two incompletes and graduated), I sold my van, stashed my bong, cut my hair, bought a suit, and began my career with a major stock brokerage firm. In the ensuing years, I continued down that path— ultimately forming my own investment advisory company in 1996. In all, I spent thirty-two years as a wealth management adviser, helping my clients build and preserve wealth.

At the outset, I was unaware of how much selling was involved. I was ready to put my six months of experience to work at growing *portfolios*—groupings of financial assets such as stocks, bonds, and cash. Instead, I had to pick up the phone, call strangers, and convince them that their money was better off with me captaining their ship than their current broker with thirty years' experience. That's selling, and it's not easy. But I loved it.

Equally important, I needed to perform for my clients. I had to deliver on what I had sold them on. That way, I could be confident that clients would be coming in the door faster than they were leaving.

As my career progressed, I realized that, in many cases, an individual's investment decisions were driven not by knowledge but by emotions and feel (think blackjack). Often an individual isn't aware of the feelings, fears, and attitudes that influence their decisions. To help my clients overcome these hurdles and make the right decisions, I boned up on psychology, something I hadn't studied since my undergraduate days. That made me a better financial adviser and an even better salesman. In 2012, I was fortunate to sell my advisory business, and I began coaching executives and business owners to become more effective in their respective fields.

The investment world is rife with conflicts of interest. More specifically, what is good for the adviser isn't necessarily suitable for the client. In this book, I will examine the pervasive smoke and mirrors I have witnessed over my career in the financial arena. Sharing the knowledge I have acquired to benefit the average investor is now my mission, and this book is one way I can fulfill that calling. In it, I will show you how to reach your financial goals—what to do and, perhaps more importantly, what not to do. While experience may be a good teacher, many of the mistakes people make with their financial planning are the result of poor preparation, hasty decisions, or outright carelessness. These mistakes can cost you plenty. Learning from someone else's experience, when possible, is usually a good idea.

Like most people, you have probably met some of your financial goals, perhaps starting a savings account or owning your own home (at least a piece of it). Still, other milestones likely remain seemingly beyond your financial reach. The fact that you are reading these words is indicative of your desire to get a better grip on managing your money. The ultimate goal of financial planning for most people—and probably you—is to ensure a comfortable and dignified retirement.

There are two potential outcomes for your retirement. You outlive your money, or your money outlasts you. In a world where people have ever-increasing life spans, accumulating enough money these days to retire with financial dignity is a challenge. Not too long ago, people retired at sixty and died at sixty-three. That didn't take a lot of planning. Nowadays, many people spend as much time in retirement as they did at work. To quote Shakespeare, "there's the rub." My path from neophyte to a financial expert is a road you can choose to travel down as well. If you begin making better decisions now, it shouldn't take you nearly as long as it did me. The journey for you starts where you are right now and hopefully ends with you enjoying a comfortable retirement.

I have made many savvy decisions on behalf of my clients, as well as for myself. However, I would argue that there is more to glean from the bad ones, and I have certainly made more than my fair share of bone-headed moves. Through trial and error over more than thirty years, I have learned what works and what does not.

Intelligent investing, much like basic strategy in blackjack, is genuinely not that complicated. The behemoth of the financial services industry makes investing appear complicated, manufacturing an artificial need for assistance and separating investors from their hard-earned dollars, all while offering little in return beyond providing an entertaining place to play—much like a casino does. There are plenty of exceptions, but many brokers and so-called Wall Street experts do not necessarily have your best interests in mind. Awareness of this inherent conflict of interest can help you avoid the inevitable obstacles and pitfalls that will present themselves along the way.

When I began my career, there was no internet, no CNBC, no ticker running across the bottom of the TV, and no discount brokers. *Money* magazine was just getting off the ground. The full-service broker was essentially the only game in town. We took full advantage of the situation, charging 2 percent on every stock trade—both the buy and the sell. We sold *mutual funds*—a financial vehicle made up of a pool of money collected from many investors to invest in securities like stocks, bonds, and money market accounts—with 8.5 percent commissions. As the business evolved along with the technology underpinning it, trading commissions have come down to virtually zero, and no-load (no commission) mutual funds are ubiquitous.

Despite this trend toward reducing the cost of doing business, Wall Street continues to thrive. Investment firms and their advisers are continually reinventing themselves while struggling to provide value for the fees they charge. There seems to be a financial adviser on every corner these days, touting the next new product as the panacea for all our economic ills. My automobile insurance agent wants my IRA business. The next thing you know, my dry cleaner will want to trade *options*—complex financial derivatives that I suggest you avoid—for me. Sadly, most of these "experts" have no idea what the hell they're doing.

Despite all the distractions, the proper path may be boring and not serve you particularly well when it comes to entertaining cocktail conversation. Listening to the media or Uncle Louie's hot stock tip is simply noise that you should, for the most part, ignore. There is certainly nothing wrong with a little "action" now and then, provided you take the necessary time to learn the rules of engagement prior to battle and are willing to take your chances.

It's time to put an intelligent, unemotional, cost-effective, efficient strategy to work.

I'm going to lay it all out for you and trust that you will take action. The following fifty-two chapters—a full deck—deal with *mindset, knowledge,* and *execution.*

The Mindset section is about you and what's between your ears—call it a brief course on the psychology of money. You will be encouraged to employ the most rigorous honesty you can muster about your relationship with money. Achieving this level of virtue is a challenging endeavor you may find uncomfortable, but without coming clean (at least to yourself), the remaining pages will be of little use. Before you can effectively process the knowledge required to execute an effective financial plan, there's some rewiring to be done. Many of the beliefs you consider sacrosanct will lead to faulty thinking. Perhaps your assumptions are just dated or, worse, completely misleading. Nonetheless, you must begin this exploration with an open mind.

In the Knowledge section, I will examine the investment landscape—the good, the bad, and the ugly. Once you understand what you need to know and what you can (thankfully) discard, you can begin to develop a thirty-thousand-foot view of your financial picture. By the time you complete this section, you will have reassessed your mindset, had a few epiphanies along the way, acquired a bit of knowledge, and be ready to put your game plan into action. With the clarity that comes as a result, you can begin to move forward with execution.

The Execution section is about putting your newfound knowledge to work. If you eat well and exercise regularly, you know what results to expect. If you smoke three packs of cigarettes a day, drink to excess, and eat crappy food, you also know where that will lead. This knowledge, sadly, doesn't necessarily translate to healthy eating and getting to the gym. I know from my coaching experience that most people have a pretty good idea of what to do, yet they just don't do it.

I love storytelling and have used short stories to share my expertise with you. This style of writing will hopefully be entertaining and resonate in such a way that you won't get lost in the weeds. But don't let this approach fool you into thinking this book doesn't offer solid advice. I have distilled the complex and technical nature of investing into a form that is relatively easy to follow. I've done the hard work so you can reap the benefits.

This book offers you a lot of valuable information, and by the end, it will all make sense. I will provide the roadmap designed to get you from where you are now to where you want to be—but you must take action. All the advice in the world is of no value if you fail to act. Don't be the proverbial horse that was led to water but refused to drink.

To be most effective, read this book in the order written from beginning to end. Do not jump forward to the Knowledge and Execution sections looking for that magic pill that's going to make all your financial dreams come true. You won't find it. You have to crawl before you walk. You have to walk before you run. Only then can you consider running a marathon. You must train.

At a glance, you may not think everything in this book applies to your financial situation. That's probably true. Nonetheless, I urge you to read this book in its entirety.

Take a deep breath, open your mind, purge your preconceptions about money, and be ready to challenge yourself. You will gain the knowledge you need to take control of your money. Then it all comes down to execution. I wish you all the best as you begin your financial journey.

MINDSET

CHAPTER 1

MINDFULNESS

" *Until you make the unconscious conscious, it will direct your life, and you will call it fate.*

—Carl Jung

Successful poker players have learned to be mindful. What, you may ask, does that even mean? The short answer is to be *present*. The game involves frequent swings of emotion, and stressful situations can easily throw you off your game and cause you to make poor decisions. Paying close attention to how your behavior is affected, and adjusting accordingly, is key to honing your skills as a poker player. Ditto when it comes to your money.

Like an alcoholic beginning a twelve-step program to recovery, the journey to financial well-being starts with admitting that much of what you have been doing hasn't panned out so well. Often, it's been nothing short of disastrous. You may have heard the saying that insanity is doing the same thing over and over again and expecting different results. We are all guilty of committing the same mistakes and hoping that the next time will be different. Moving forward, however, requires acknowledging that what hasn't worked for you so far isn't going help you meet your goals. Change is necessary if you want something to improve, and that is certainly true when it comes to mindset.

Many of your decisions are the result of being hardwired to think a certain way. This wiring is deeply embedded in your psyche, steering your thinking on a subconscious level—even if it's inherently flawed. The subconscious mind cannot distinguish between fact and fiction, creating all sorts of problems. When your head is full of unsubstantiated beliefs, those beliefs dictate your behavior without you so much as questioning them, which is the polar opposite of mindfulness.

Your past money mistakes don't have to define your future. It's never too late to right your ship and design a future that offers the promise of a comfortable life. There are countless stories of people who have been in dire situations and made massive life changes to rally and finish strong. I know these people exist because I'm one of them.

If you were fortunate to be raised by successful parents, perhaps you have emulated your parents' behavior and learned effective money-management habits at an early age. As a result, you made a lot, saved a lot, invested it well, and then inherited a lot—but perhaps something still feels off-kilter. Ask yourself this: Do you own your money, or does money own you? The latter is no way to live.

Perhaps you were significantly less advantaged. Your parents were unable to teach you proper money-management strategies because they never learned any themselves. Instead, they may have passed along their ineffectual financial tactics, fears, and attitudes. The lack of money carries with it a lot of embarrassment and shame, and this can flow down from generation to generation. As a result, financial struggles are not discussed. Perhaps you created your own rules to avoid the economic chaos of your childhood. Maybe you exhibit all the outward signs of monetary well-being but are, in reality, drowning in debt to keep up with the Joneses. Do you continually purchase things you don't need, with money you don't have, to impress people you don't even like? Now that's insanity.

You might be young and just starting in life. If so, count yourself lucky. Your mind may not yet be crammed full of misinformation and bad habits, and time is indeed your friend. I wish I had known and done what I'm sharing in this book when I was in my twenties.

Every one of us has a conversation with our money. Regardless of your station in life and financial acumen, there is always room for improvement. Many basic tenets have endured for generations, but some are fluid and change over time. What worked well in the past is not guaranteed to do so in the future.

As you get older, your financial priorities will undoubtedly change. Life happens. Someday you will want to retire, but the day that you decide or have to stop work could very well come sooner rather than later. There is always the possibility that an unexpected life event, such as an unfortunate accident, will leave you unable to generate income to prepare for retirement. In life, sudden and unplanned expenses are almost a certainty. With all the what-ifs out there, you should strive to prepare for every potential scenario that might come your way. Taking good care of your money is central to this planning.

All this begins with being willing to have those tough conversations regarding your finances. Money is a tool, a means to an end—not an end unto itself. The unprepared and those without a sound financial plan often wake up worrying about how to get more money or how to keep from frittering away the money they have. That is no way for anyone to live. Stop stressing about money, and spend time learning how to make money work for you instead of against you. Then you can go about enjoying your life. It's not enough to want to change your financial status. You have to do your homework, put a plan in place, and then stick with the program.

Rigorously examine where your behaviors regarding money have led you astray.

Make a list of words and phrases that describe your experience with money.

What actions can you take to change those behaviors that have not worked well for you?

Take care of your money,

and it will take care of you.

CHAPTER 2

TO THINE OWN SELF BE TRUE

Sometimes in order to be happy in the present moment, you have to be willing to give up all hopes for a better past.

—Robert Holden, PhD

Let's be honest—all of us have made mistakes. It's what makes us human. And I have made more mistakes than most. My twenties were tough years. With a degree in economics from Duke University, I had everything one could ask for to live a productive life and enjoy a successful career. My nature was personable, and people seemed to like me. I was smarter than the average bear, and I knew how to sell. I secured a terrific first job as a financial adviser with a major brokerage house. I was on my way, but I had one big problem to overcome.

Alcohol.

I won't entertain or horrify you with my numerous war stories, but it wasn't pretty. I wanted to make as much money as I could, and I would say and do whatever it took to make it happen. Although my clients were always important to me, my personal needs and wants often took priority. I was anything but authentic, and nobody should have trusted me—certainly not with their money. Even though I was making better money than most of my peers, I was spending even more and piling up ridiculous amounts of debt. It became hard to breathe whenever I thought about it.

It was a hellish existence. As my life continued down a road to ruin, I was fortunate to realize that as long as I kept drinking, my station in life wasn't going to improve. I had to make what amounted to a life-and-death decision. On July 20, 1986, I quit drinking for good. If someone had asked me back then whether I thought I could go a whole year without a drink, I would have told them I had a better chance at taking Michael Jordan's place with the Chicago Bulls. But here I am today with over thirty-four years of sobriety. Miracles do happen.

My sobriety is not a source of pride. Instead, I am simply full of gratitude. I am one of the lucky ones. I learned how to live one day at a time. The past was not going to change, no matter how hard I tried, and the future was uncertain. All I was capable of managing was the present, and that was a full-time job.

I look at goal setting in a similar fashion. Having clarified my medium- and long-term goals, I devised a simple, concise blueprint for my day and continued to keep my focus on what was right in front of me. This sea change began with an exercise in rigorous self-honesty. I had lied to myself for so long that none of this came quickly. But as I started down this road, I slowly but surely evolved into an entirely different kind of financial adviser. The mantra I began to practice was this: I will tell the truth, maintain integrity, and only recommend to clients that they do what I would do if I were in their situation. Initially, I left a lot of money on the table by being selfless for a change, but it worked exceedingly well for the remainder of my career.

Why am I telling you this in a book about finance? Because I now realize that putting the pieces of your financial life in order requires that you take your self-honesty to a whole new level. I also know that it's never too late to change.

Likewise, to keep from losing money in blackjack, I needed to admit my naivete and learn proper strategy. Once I became knowledgeable and understood the game fully, I found better places to put my money.

Perhaps you're nearing retirement without the resources to make that stage of your life an enjoyable one. Maybe you're living paycheck to paycheck and can't even begin to see the light at the end of the tunnel. More than likely, you'd prefer not to think about those scenarios. Perhaps you're terrified. But not thinking about your financial worries will not make them go away.

Take the time to paint a clear and concise picture of your future. Use your imagination and have some fun with this. Make a vision board if that floats your boat. There are no right answers. This part is entirely up to you. If you have a significant other, involve that person every step along the way to make sure that you're both heading in the same direction.

Change can be right around the corner. You can make it happen, but more than likely it will be a long and arduous project. I have walked that walk myself and have been instrumental in helping countless others do the same. If you have lost your self-esteem, I promise you can have it back. But it's going to take some work. Hopefully, this book will be instrumental in influencing that change

What lies have you continually told yourself?

How will it feel to take your self-honesty to a whole new level?

Change can only begin
once you learn to be honest with yourself.

CHAPTER 3

CLARITY IS POWER

" *"Would you tell me, please, which way I ought to go from here?"*

"That depends a good deal on where you want to get to," said the Cat.

"I don't much care where—" said Alice.

"Then it doesn't matter which way you go," said the Cat.

"—so long as I get SOMEWHERE," Alice added as an explanation.

"Oh, you're sure to do that," said the Cat, "if you only walk long enough."

—Lewis Carroll, from Alice's Adventures in Wonderland

We all have some experience setting goals, perhaps to lose weight, quit smoking, or make more money. Sometimes we might even succeed. But we all know how difficult attaining those goals can be. Often the lack of success in achieving a goal comes down to a lack of clarity, and a vague goal will never lead you to success.

There is much to be learned from Thomas J. Watson, the founder of IBM. He credited the success of his company to the crystal-clear picture he had of IBM as an established company when it was in its infancy. In other words, he knew exactly where his company was going long before it got there. He realized that for IBM to become a great company, it would have to act like a great company from day one. Much like navigating a ship through stormy seas, Watson and his team consistently measured the disparity between the company they had and the company they envisioned. When they found themselves off course, they made whatever adjustments were required to narrow the gap.

If you hope to succeed in any endeavor, you must take time to set realistic goals that will motivate you. Ask yourself the tough questions. Why is the result valuable and essential to you? If you have little interest in a goal's outcome, you'll likely lack the drive required to achieve it.

If you don't know where you're going, any road will take you there. What are your financial goals? Are you saving for retirement, a home purchase, college, or a wedding? When would you like to retire or be in a financial position to choose that option? Do you want to leave an *estate*—the money or property owned by you—for your children or other beneficiaries? To meet those goals, you must first calculate the specific dollar amount required and the deadline for achieving it. This book will show you how to do just that.

To implement an effective financial plan requires a high degree of clarity, and with clarity comes conviction.

On the personal front, where would you like to live? Do you enjoy traveling, and if so, where would you like to visit? Do you plan to stay active? In essence, what do you want your life to look like in your golden years?

I cannot overemphasize the importance of putting your visions down in writing. There is magic in doing so. The more detailed, the better. Get clear on where you want to go and when you want to arrive.

As a money mentor and coach, I work with my clients to clarify their visions, create a plan, and provide the accountability necessary to make sure they stay on track.

The process begins with establishing long-term and measurable goals, complete with a timeline. A goal without a due date is nothing more than a pipe dream. I then work backward and develop five-year, one-year, one-month, and daily goals.

Consider this simple daily checklist (always subject to change) I use to rate my day:

1. Get eight hours of sleep.

2. Write for a minimum of one hour.

3. Meditate.

4. Stretch/exercise.

5. Avoid sugar.

6. Be prudent with expenditures.

7. Study Spanish.

8. Read for a minimum of one hour.

9. Watch TV for a maximum of one hour.

10. Do something thoughtful for someone else.

While creating this list may seem a somewhat pedestrian exercise, working toward these ten goals helps me stay focused on what I have determined to be valuable to me. It is rare for me to achieve a perfect ten on any given day, but it does happen. Many of my coaching clients have created their daily checklist, and it's always fun to ask them what their score was for the day before.

◆

Where do you lack clarity in your life?

How would it feel to have a plan in place and know where you're going?

Put your goals in writing, complete with deadlines, and determine the activities required for you to reach them.

CHAPTER 4

WEALTH AND MONEY

" *It's good to have money and the things that money can buy, but it's good, too, to check up once in a while and make sure you haven't lost the things that money can't buy.*

—George Lorimer

The 1980s was a great time to be a stockbroker. It was the decade of yuppies (young urban professionals), and the focus was on making money. I made my share and then some, earning more than most of my friends (excluding those who went to work for Daddy), but sadly, I spent all of it and more. My "plan" was to become a millionaire by the time I was thirty, then go out and find the perfect trophy wife, and eventually have children.

So much for that.

By the time I was thirty, I had more *liabilities* (what you owe) than I had *assets* (what you own). I somehow got my trophy wife four years earlier, and we were the proud parents of a beautiful baby girl. But I had become a raging alcoholic and was on the verge of going bankrupt. My job was no longer fulfilling. With the added pressure of having a family, I was willing to say and do whatever it took to make a buck. Eventually, the day came when I could no longer look at myself in the mirror. There had to be more to life, I thought. I was smart and willing to work hard, and there had to be a way to employ those attributes to benefit those I served and not just myself. I began a new chapter by giving up alcohol and refocusing my approach in every aspect of my life. That's what I needed to do to have a fighting chance of turning my life around.

Money means different things to different people. The good news is that you get to decide for yourself the role that money plays in your life. I challenge you to step back for a moment and consider what matters most to you when it comes to money. Some people think it can make them happy, while others beg to differ. Some people boast about how much they have, while some lament the fact they have so little. Both of these conversations bore me to tears. I have better things to do with my life than to listen to a bunch of chest-pounding or whining. Don't waste your time with these people. They won't do you any good.

Prevailing "wisdom" suggests that wealth means having lots of money. When you see someone who lives in an opulent mansion, drives an exotic automobile, wears elegant clothes, and only dines at five-star restaurants, you probably would categorize that person as wealthy. But is that real wealth? That may indeed be your definition—and it was undoubtedly mine at one time—but the older (and hopefully wiser) I have become, the more I have questioned this widely held convention. I have managed money for many "wealthy" individuals who were, truth be known, miserable human beings. At the other end of the spectrum, I know many people who, while living paycheck to paycheck, live happy existences full of meaning and purpose. An old friend of mine once told me he would consider himself successful when he could, with no thought of the cost, afford to fly first class and dine at any restaurant he fancied. If that is what rocks your world, I am not going to judge.

Throughout my life, I have reevaluated my definition of wealth on more than one occasion. For me, wealth is the freedom that comes from having enough money to do what I want to do without spending much time thinking about whether I can afford it. The less I have to worry about money, the happier I am.

Of course, you must secure the physiological needs required for survival. It's hard to be happy with no roof over your head or food in your belly. To be reliant on family or the government to satisfy those needs, if you are genuinely in a position to fend for yourself, is both unfair and shameful. I'm not belittling the importance of money—we all need it to live—but how much you need is entirely up to you.

Decide to take control of your money rather than have it control you. Money controlled much of my life for way too long, but over the years, I have slowly but surely taken back control. Given the fact that you are holding this book in your hands, it's safe to say that we are on the same page.

The Bible says that the love of money is the root of all evil, and some people misinterpret that to mean that money itself is evil. There's nothing sinister about gainful employment or using the money you've earned to secure your future and provide for your loved ones. Living in poverty is not sanctimonious. Money is only valuable because of what it can purchase; it is not an end unto itself. You may have all the toys that money can buy and still feel that something is missing. Perhaps your pursuit of the almighty dollar has caused you to neglect other areas of your life—spending time with family, taking care of your health, and enjoying doing the things that light your fire.

If I had to highlight the most significant success of my life, it would be the fact that I raised three wonderful daughters, each on the road to success on their terms. No amount of money is more important to me than that. But that's just me. What about you?

How would it feel if you could spend less time worrying about your money and more time living your life?

Define wealth on your terms.

CHAPTER 5

THE STICKINESS FACTOR

> *I'm thankful for the three-ounce Ziploc bag so I have somewhere to put my savings.*
>
> —Paula Poundstone

Here's a great example of what not to do.

Archie Karas is considered by many to be the most notorious gambler in the history of Las Vegas. Karas grew up poor in Greece and immigrated to the United States, determined to find a better life. Initially, he waited tables in a restaurant and hustled locals in an adjacent pool hall when he wasn't working. His penchant for playing games and gambling made his transition to poker a natural one. Within just a few months, he had accumulated a bankroll of $2 million. A year later, it was all gone. Broke, but not ready to call it a day, he convinced a friend to loan him

$10,000 to play in a poker game. He promptly turned that loan into $30,000. His reputation as a shrewd poker player had made finding a backer not that difficult. After repaying the loan, Karas increased his winnings to over $1 million by shooting pool. He then went on to upend many of the best poker players around at the time. He got on a roll at the craps table (pun intended). His winning streak went on for three years, culminating in an astounding bankroll of $40 million.

Subsequently, he paid a visit to Lyle Berman, a member of the Poker Hall of Fame and an extraordinarily successful businessman, and asked what he should do with the money. Berman advised Karas to purchase an *immediate annuity*—a guaranteed insurance product that would provide him with an income of $200,000 a month and leave his principle of $40 million intact. He asked Berman if the income was taxable and was told that it was indeed. Well, Karas wanted no part of that and refused to take Berman's sage advice. Two years later, all the money had been redistributed into other people's wallets, and Karas continued his life working at the Golden Nugget as a coat checker.

You may not know someone as flamboyant as Karas, but we all know people who can't get ahead financially no matter how much money they make. People with salaries more than sufficient to cover the necessities and fund the occasional splurge should seemingly have plenty of money left over to invest for future needs. Instead, many end up barely getting by. Lottery winners, professional athletes, and celebrities frequently end up destitute.

How does that happen?

The way I see it is that some people simply aren't comfortable with having money. To them, money exists only to be spent, and it can sure be spent in a hurry. Studies show that lottery winners often become depressed, and their relationships with family and friends suffer. Financial windfalls can lead to divorce, alcohol and drug problems, and even suicide. Lottery winners frequently blow through their money quickly with little thought of investing even a sliver of their winnings toward retirement savings to secure their futures.

Here's a windfall for you to ponder. A former employee of mine inherited $100,000. She and her husband were people of modest means, yet they promptly purchased matching Hummers and became the talk of the town, and not in glowing terms. There was no thought given to the cost of maintenance, property taxes, or depreciation—not to mention the gas! They were in their thirties at the time, and that windfall could have jump-started their retirement fund significantly. I should have fired her on the grounds of stupidity.

On the other end of the spectrum, some people prefer saving, quietly investing an appropriate percentage of their income consistently. They have conditioned themselves over time to be good stewards of their money, even if they never made the big bucks.

Larry Fitzgerald, the exceptional and highly paid NFL receiver, understands well the benefits of delayed gratification and has, as a result, amassed a net worth of nearly $100 million. He once said in an interview that he prefers to spend his money on things he expects to go up in value. What a novel concept. Sometimes the greatest truths are the simplest.

The winners in the money game have different mind-sets when it comes to living within their means and forgoing instant gratification. If they are fortunate enough to receive a financial windfall like an inheritance, they don't rush out and buy a bigger house or a fancier car. Instead, they see the opportunity to supplement their retirement planning by putting that money to work. If you have a history of letting money slip through your hands such that your comfortable retirement appears to be in jeopardy, it's time to develop a different set of habits.

How much money has passed through your hands during your lifetime?

What percentage of that money have you saved?

How would you handle a windfall like an inheritance?

If money hasn't stuck to you in the past, make the decision right now to get sticky.

CHAPTER 6

BEANS

" *A man is rich in proportion to the number of things he can let alone.*

—Henry David Thoreau

When I was a stockbroker in the '80s, the business was all about cold-calling. Long before there was a Do Not Call Registry, I stayed on the phone all day, calling strangers with high-paying jobs and big houses in upscale neighborhoods. I did my best to convince them to buy whatever was in vogue that day and then crossed my fingers that the check would arrive by settlement date.

One day, following my monthly ritual of sending out ten thousand prospecting mailers, I received a reply card back from a man named Beans. (I'm not making this up.) He was from a rural community in eastern North Carolina, and I had a limited partnership available. During our call, he mentioned that he had $30,000 he might be willing to invest, and, in those days, the commission was a whopping 8 percent, or $2,400, with my cut being 40 percent. A successful sale would put almost a thousand dollars in my pocket. So, I jumped in my car and headed to Mayberry.

When I pulled up in front of the house, I was sure that I had the wrong address or that someone had played a prank on me. I stared at the modest ranch house (my use of the word *modest* here is a stretch), which sat behind an array of tacky yard art, pink flamingos, and a rusted-out automobile perched atop concrete blocks. There was no way the people who lived in this house had that kind of money, but the drive had been over two hours, and I had nothing to lose by knocking on the door. If nothing else, it might be entertaining.

A man I presumed to be in his early seventies, dressed in a stained white T-shirt and a pair of old jeans, welcomed me into his humble abode. Although it was not yet lunchtime, he offered me a beer—Black Label, as low-end as it gets. Truthfully, I was more of a Heineken kind of guy, but beer is beer, and I didn't want to appear rude. (This was before I gave up alcohol.) The inside of the house was as unpretentious as the outside. The furniture could have been in the Smithsonian. It was dated and shoddy, and I can still remember the unpleasant, musty odor.

Beans and his wife could not have been a sweeter couple. We sat down at the dining room table, and I dove into my sales presentation. Everything was progressing nicely, and they indicated some level of interest. Their investment experience was limited to their previous company's stock and a savings account at the local bank. It would be a big step, they told me, to proceed with the investment. Then Beans pulled out their bank statement.

I nearly fell off my chair.

They had close to $1 million in their previous employer's stock and another $1.2 million sitting in a passbook savings account at their local bank! I couldn't contain myself. "Where did you get all this money?" I had to ask. My mind was racing. They didn't appear to be the drug-smuggling types, and I sat on my hands to keep them from shaking while I waited for their response.

The two of them had worked for a large company (at the time, one of the Dow 30) for thirty-five years. Neither had graduated from high school, and they were not particularly well-paid employees. Beans was something akin to a janitor, and his wife held a low-paying clerical position. They had recently retired, having earned a combined $70,000 in their final year. It just didn't add up.

The sparks began to fly between them as they argued vehemently about the size of the initial monthly investment they had made in their company stock. She claimed it was $5, and he was adamant that it was $10. I later looked at the long-term performance chart of the stock, and it was decent but far from outstanding. It was no Microsoft. How was it possible that they had amassed such a sum? Maybe they were in the drug business after all. But as the discussion ensued, I learned that their strategy was an inherently simple one.

When they received a raise, if only a few dollars a month, they invested the full increase in their company's stock or added it to their savings account at the bank. Over time, that sum grew to a healthy seven figures. Incredibly, they never invested in any other stocks or higher-yielding investments. Had they done that, their bank account might have had an additional zero or two. I realize this is an extreme example, but it illustrates a fundamental truth in investing. A slow-and-steady strategy does indeed work over the long haul, and you don't need to be a genius to adopt one.

While some people might regard them as cheap, the simple truth is that Beans and his wife never bought into the typical American ideal of consumerism. They saw no need to use every increase in pay they received to buy a bigger house, a fancier car, or more expensive clothes. They were happily married—going on forty-five years— and more than content living in their bucolic little town. I would consider them to be a wealthy couple regardless of their impressive financial statement.

I have known many people that, although they live in large homes and drive the best automobiles, worry about money daily. The relationships with their children are all but nonexistent, and many of them couldn't write a check for $10,000 that would clear the bank. Wealth has a funny way of hiding out in the most unlikely of places.

I'd like to say that I learned a valuable lesson during the Beans experience and traded in my Heineken for Black Label, but I had certain standards to uphold.

◆

How can you apply the story of Beans to modify your financial mindset?

Can you accept the idea that it's possible to reach your financial goals even if you don't make a lot of money?

Given time, even a modest income can provide for a sweet retirement.

CHAPTER 7

DEVELOPING BETTER HABITS

> " *People do not decide their futures; they decide their habits, and their habits decide their future.*
>
> —F. M. Alexander

It's time for you to develop some better habits, discarding the bad ones, and picking up some good ones. Harness whatever inner motivation you require to make the changes you need to make.

Habits have a way of compounding—excellent news for your good habits, but not so much for your bad ones. The results are often not immediate. For example, it might take weeks or even months for your hard work in a new exercise program to pay off. But if you put in the work, the results will come. Furthermore, if your goal is to lose weight, you might consider visiting the healthier areas of your favorite grocery store for a change. Those donuts add up over time.

In my early days of playing poker, I had a bad habit of making ridiculous bluffs just to see if I could get away with it. It was a significant boost to my ego when the other players would fold their cards when I had nothing. Often I would show my bluff just to send a signal to the table that I was a force to be reckoned with and that they needed to take me seriously. Over time, I learned that continuing to play that way would lead me to the poor house. Bad habit identified. Bad habit eliminated.

All of us are creatures of habit, and you might as well make that work to your benefit. For me, it is easier to ditch a bad habit by replacing it with a good one. This concept may seem elementary, but it works.

The subconscious mind can play a lot of tricks on you. For example, my golf game is better when I focus on hitting my tee shot down the middle of the fairway rather than focusing on avoiding the woods. If my subconscious is dwelling on the trees, my golf ball has a way of finding them. It's about mindset. If I think long enough about not doing something, I tend to end up doing it.

If you want to take charge of your finances, make time to write down your good habits, bad habits, and the changes you need to make.

If procrastination is one of your albatrosses, you have plenty of company. You might be able to justify procrastination in the short term, but you will more than likely pay dearly for it in the long run. It's rarely a problem doing what's in our long-term best interest as long as it feels right today. But when the activities staring us in the face are unpleasant, requiring effort or sacrifice, the procrastination monster rears its ugly head and tells us we can put off until later. Behavioral scientists call this *present bias*.

The fact is this kind of future-planning is easy to put off. The immediate pleasure often exerts a more substantial influence on decision-making than the satisfaction derived from working toward long-term goals. That intoxicating new-car smell can easily make one neglect the reality of five years of monthly payments, plus interest, on a depreciating asset. Immediate gratification quickly diverts money away from the pursuit of a healthy financial future. The mind can be a terrible thing if you don't rein it in occasionally. Beware the long-term consequences of short-term behavior.

How can you shake the costly habit of procrastination? I have learned from my own experience—and from helping others implement changes—that willpower, while an admirable trait, invariably falls short of the mark. The only successful technique I have found to deal with procrastination is to develop *systems* and then adhere to them. This book outlines a proven method to help make your financial goals become a reality. Whether or not you put the system to work is up to you. Be the person who does instead of the person who just talks, and your behavior will begin to align with your newfound knowledge and discipline.

When it comes to planning your financial future, the sooner you begin to execute, the more likely you are to achieve your goals.

If you have a recurring task that you never seem to get to or always put on the backburner, place those tasks on autopilot, if possible. This process will go a long way toward ensuring that what needs to get done gets done. The use of systems is often misconstrued as being unnecessarily complicated when, ironically, they offer ways to simplify your life.

Give up trying to control the results because that won't work. Instead, focus on what you can manage in the here and now. Allow the results to happen in their own time. Meeting long-term goals requires short-term execution.

This shift in focus has been a painful life lesson for me to learn, but it has certainly made my life a lot less stressful.

Certain activities cannot wait. You must act on them beginning today, not tomorrow. Time is an indispensable asset that needs to work in your favor, not against you, making procrastination a luxury you cannot afford.

Begin by adopting *time blocking*, where you set aside a time—perhaps two hours a month—to sit quietly without distractions and deal with your money matters. This simple habit is essential and will produce fruit, helping you know what other actions need to be implemented and maintained consistently. Be present. Refer to this book as a guide. Learn to be mindful. When you master time with good habits and productive systems, you master your money.

Where have your bad habits led you astray?

What benefits can you derive from replacing certain bad habits with good ones?

The instant gratification of self-control can be exhilarating.

CHAPTER 8

I WANT IT NOW

> *Because money permits a constant stream of luxuries and indulgences, it can take away their savor, and by permitting instant gratification, money shortcuts the happiness of anticipation. Scrimping, saving, imagining, planning, hoping—these stages enlarge the happiness we feel.*
>
> —Gretchen Rubin

Unskilled poker players often exhibit impatience instead of letting the game come to them. They crave the adrenaline rush, and that mindset can be costly.

There is a well-known study of instant gratification that was conducted by Stanford University in the late 1960s and early 1970s. Children had to choose between an immediate and small reward, such as a marshmallow or a cookie, or a more substantial treat fifteen minutes later. The children who managed to wait longer tended to have better outcomes, as evidenced in later years by their SAT scores, educational attainment, body mass index, and other life measures. Affluence and age, not willpower, explained the results. Further follow-up studies demonstrated that those who opted for delayed gratification were more likely to achieve success later in life.

The inclination to choose immediate gratification is universal and can show up in any area of your life. For example, perhaps you promise yourself that you'll make increasing your savings a priority. Then you see a new lens for your camera and decide to splurge, telling yourself you'll make the expense up next month. As a result, your savings dwindle rather than grow. While typically occurring at a subconscious level, the long-term effects of short-term decisions based on immediate gratification can be profound. To better understand your money behaviors, take a fearless and moral inventory of the financial decisions you've made in the past. Every dollar you spend reflects a battle between the instant gratification monkey and the rational decision-maker. Suppose you spend the money you're saving up for a dream vacation on a new outfit, knowing full well you can't afford both. A little discipline and patience here can go a long way toward achieving your financial goals. The small sacrifices you make along the way will generate big payoffs down the road.

In the United States, enough money passes through most people's hands during their lifetimes for them to accumulate a respectable sum, one that would ensure a comfortable retirement. But our culture is one of pervasive consumption, continually bombarding us with messages designed to convince us that we need or deserve certain material things to be happy. The happiness derived from such purchases is fleeting at best. There are countless benefits to incorporating the practice of delayed gratification into your life. While your net worth will certainly appreciate your efforts, creating good habits and exercising self-discipline will also boost your self-esteem. The best investment advice is worthless when you don't have any money left over at the end of the day to put to work for your future. To create a habit of delayed gratification, consider implementing the following strategies:

♣ Determine what is most important to you and your life.

♣ Define your goals and map out a plan to achieve them.

♣ Develop an awareness of trade-offs as they occur, understanding that the dollar you spend today is worth much more when compounded over your lifetime.

♣ Avoid impulse purchases.

♣ Make better choices.

I'm not suggesting that you become a tightwad. Just be a little more mindful for a change. You will be astonished when you realize how little you need to give up to achieve your goals. And by all means, reward yourself when you reach a goal. You deserve a little fun along the way.

♦

How has succumbing to immediate gratification in the past affected your current financial situation?

What would your financial life look like now had you exercised more discipline and avoided impulsive purchases?

Beware the long-term consequences of short-term behavior.

CHAPTER 9

PAPER OR PLASTIC?

Actions speak louder than words and not nearly as often.

—Mark Twain

If you're like most people, you regularly carry multiple payment options in your wallet. I understand the need for credit cards, but is it necessary to have so many? They can make spending money quick and easy. Maybe too easy.

Casinos use chips for a reason. Tossing a hundred-dollar chip into a pot is a lot easier than throwing in a hundred-dollar bill. Once players exchange their money for chips, most will spend all their chips rather than cash in the remainder at the cashier window, which is always tricky to find, especially after all the free drinks. These financial proxies say a lot about how we view our money. The more that purveyors of goods and services can distance us from the reality that our cash is changing hands, the more likely we are to part with our dough. If you believe a spending problem may be keeping you from achieving your goals, you need to take a hard look at how you spend your money.

One way to see exactly where your money is going is to try using cash for a few weeks. Chances are you will be a more conscious spender. The immediacy of a cash transaction, in contrast to the deferred payment of a credit card, forces you to make better, more prudent choices. Watching your stack of bills dwindle at an alarming rate can make you think long and hard before you hand over five dollars for a designer coffee every day. The cash-only experiment will teach you invaluable lessons about how easily you can be convinced to spend.

My children find it hilarious that I continue to use cash for most of my smaller purchases. They, on the other hand, never seem to have a dollar bill or a quarter in their pocket when they need one, but they have plenty of plastic. They are always surprised and dismayed at the end of the month when they receive their credit card bills. *How could I have possibly spent that much money?* Thankfully, there's a minimum payment option.

I accept the fait accompli that cash is going the way of the dinosaur. Undoubtedly, the day will come when we will make all of our purchases digitally. I enjoy being one of the last holdouts, and I'm going down fighting because I'm old and stubborn. Not to mention, it's fun to give my kids something to laugh about every once in a while.

But don't think I universally despise credit cards. Cash is not always an option. When it comes to online shopping, credit cards typically offer more fraud protection than debit cards (although debit card transactions are beginning to receive similar protections). With hacking and mining for personal information on the rise, a little protection is more than warranted.

Many credit cards offer cash back or travel miles as perks. These perks should not be an incentive to spend foolishly, but free is free. While department store credit cards may offer specials and incentives, there is something to be said for the simplicity of having only one or two cards. For one thing, it's easier to monitor two cards, and it's easier to keep your spending from getting out of control. If your credit permits, secure a credit card with perks you can use.

If you have a business, it's a good idea to have a separate credit card for business use only. Pay off the balance every month and continue to live within your means.

Another benefit of credit and debit cards is the electronic record they provide of your purchases. This accounting is helpful in accurately tracking your expenses and potential tax deductions. Using a debit card should be limited to small purchases from local vendors because it costs vendors less to process debit cards. If you haven't yet qualified for a credit card, a debit card can be an obtainable electronic payment option.

◆

Do you pay off your credit card in full every month, or are your debts piling up?

Review your current assortment of credit cards and take the scissors to the ones you don't need.

Try a cash-only experiment for a week to see if that curbs your spending.

Start paying attention
to how you spend your money.

CHAPTER 10

NOT JUST A RIVER IN EGYPT

> " *Most men would rather deny a hard truth than face it.*
>
> —George R. R. Martin

Denial is the failure to acknowledge or admit into consciousness an unacceptable truth or emotion. It is exceedingly difficult for most people to recognize their bad habits in the first place, and often that is manifested in the management of their money. Denial is a defense mechanism, and denying that those bad habits exist is an all-too-frequent roadblock to financial success.

This kind of denial is prevalent among alcoholics and addicts. Those in twelve-step programs learn that owning up to having a problem is the first step, and you cannot effectively complete the steps that follow without taking this step of acknowledgment. Rarely a day goes by that I don't call on the Serenity Prayer: "God, grant me the serenity to accept the things I cannot change, courage to change the things I can, and wisdom to know the difference." So simple yet so profound. A twelve-step program requires an extensive introspection with rigorous honesty—not an easy undertaking for an alcoholic. But again, if it were easy, everyone with an alcohol problem would do it. The same goes for people struggling to save for the future.

Some people are born with certain advantages. They have educated, successful parents with above-average intelligence and solid parenting skills. On the other hand, some are born into abject poverty in an environment that encourages dependence and fosters blame. Dispense with those qualifiers and accept the fact that where you are today is primarily the result of the decisions you have made. There's no going back and rewriting the past, but you can learn from what's happened in your life and make changes going forward to achieve the outcome you want. Find the courage to act on the recommendations in this book that pertain to your situation, and have the wisdom to know the difference between what you can and cannot change.

If you're like most people, you've had some failures. Often people feel shame when things don't work out as planned, and to avoid that shame, they make excuses for the collapse. You must acknowledge and learn from your mistakes rather than pretending they never happened. Sitting on your pity potty won't help you. When a reporter asked Thomas Edison how it felt to fail a thousand times before inventing the light bulb, he responded by telling him that his invention required a thousand steps. That's a winning mindset.

In poker, everyone is effectively dealt the same cards over time. Height, weight, speed, and jumping ability are inconsequential. With no discernible advantage there, how is it that certain players continue to prosper? It certainly helps to get dealt good cards, but more important is how well you play the cards in your hand.

When Chris Moneymaker won the Main Event at the World Series of Poker in 2003 and pocketed $2.5 million for his efforts, he ushered in a new era in the world of poker. With his meager investment of $86 in an online poker room, he won the $10,000 entry fee to his first live tournament. This unlikely feat sent a clear signal to the world that anybody was capable of winning. The popularity of poker took off and continues to soar. I'm not suggesting that you should pick up poker. Instead, I am encouraging you to accept the fact that, regardless of your circumstances, you can win the game of achieving financial freedom.

All of us are in denial about something. Gamblers routinely boast about their winning sessions while denying their losing sessions ever happened. The best strategy I know of for combatting denial is to recognize it when it comes. Acknowledge it for what it is, thank it for sharing, and continue about your business. Learn to laugh at yourself.

Some people prefer not to look at the facts, but pretending that a problem doesn't exist won't make it go away. I have seen people do their grocery shopping in a convenience store with food stamps. Talk about a waste of money.

Conversely, I have witnessed seemingly well-to-do people shopping at Dollar Tree and Costco. Freeing up some extra coin to invest in growing your assets will almost certainly require you to change some spending habits. Just because your coworker or neighbor bought a new car doesn't mean you need to follow suit.

Financial prosperity is available to all of us. The first step involves taking a hard look at how you handle money and being honest about any bad habits in play. Most people would rather listen to fingernails dragged down a chalkboard instead of scrutinizing their money-handling practices. It's much easier to keep the details in the dark and hope everything will work out OK.

Regardless of where you are financially at this moment, there is always room for improvement. Take responsibility for your present circumstances and decide to implement change. For some of you, making minor changes will be sufficient, while others will need a massive overhaul. Putting the right actions in place today can yield reliable, positive results for your financial future.

Where have you found yourself in denial?

What benefits can you envision if you are willing to be rigorously honest with yourself and acknowledge how denial has negatively affected your financial well-being?

Pinpoint where you are in denial and refuse to let it dictate your decisions.

CHAPTER 11

THE DEATH KNELL OF EMOTIONS

> *The degree of one's emotions varies inversely with one's knowledge of the facts.*
>
> —Bertrand Russell

As best I can remember, every emotional decision I have ever made regarding money I came to regret. Emotions are the primary catalyst for making poor decisions. Are you trying to recoup your losses overnight? There's an entire city built upon that stratagem. Having spent more than my fair share of time at poker tables in Las Vegas, I can attest to the never-ending challenge of harnessing your emotions when those inevitable downtrends come. Stuff happens.

In poker parlance, a *bad beat* occurs when a player loses a hand in which he was an overwhelming statistical favorite. Often there is a lot of money at stake. It's painful, and it happens to every player from time to time. After a bad beat, many players will go on *tilt*—poker slang to describe the angry or frustrated emotional state of a player. This emotional state can cloud judgment and cause a player to abandon prudent strategies for reckless behavior, often with dire consequences.

Emotions are not your friends when it comes to investing either. During periods of rising markets, emotions are typically positive, and risk becomes a secondary issue or entirely forgotten. When the air escapes the balloon and the market inevitably retreats, people tend to overcompensate and become more averse to risk. This characteristic of investor psychology can lead you to adopt a more parsimonious approach to investing. These are essential psychological issues you need account for because they can skew your thinking, spawning emotions that make you feel bulletproof at market tops and paranoid at market bottoms, which is precisely the opposite of how you should act.

Let's face it. Not every investment you make is going to turn out to be the next Apple or Amazon. Despite your best efforts and in-depth research, even the most well-considered investments can go south. When those times come, and they almost certainly will, it is vital to recognize what's happening and not allow your emotions to fuel further losses. Emotions are the death knell of investing and counterproductive in making sound decisions, often encouraging the investor to sell at the bottom and buy at the top.

The specific investment strategies covered later in this book are designed to mitigate emotional attachment by following a proven system of investing.

Avoid making any investment decisions until the emotional fog has lifted, and your mind is clear. If it is necessary for you to "get up from the table," then do so. Don't compound a painful loss by throwing good money after bad. Learning to be stoic in times of emotional turmoil reaps enormous rewards over the long haul.

◆

What financial decisions have you made that were driven by emotion and not logic?

What can you do to keep from going on tilt and making bad decisions going forward?

Emotions have no place in a sound investment program.

CHAPTER 12

AVOIDING THE HERD

> *The whole problem with the world is that fools and fanatics are always so certain of themselves, and wiser people so full of doubts.*
>
> —Bertrand Russell

Throughout history, investors have fallen prey to *herd mentality*, a term describing how people can be influenced by their peers to adopt certain behaviors, often on an emotional rather than rational basis. Also known as mob mentality, pack mentality, and the madness of crowds, this collective erasure of rationality has left its mark on some of the biggest money grabs in history.

In the seventeenth century, tulip mania sent prices for tulip bulbs so high that wealthy people were trading their houses for just one or two of them. Prices dropped by 99 percent in only two days after a single buyer failed to show up for his purchase. The bubble had burst.

In the 1920s, Charles Ponzi bilked many Italian immigrants out of millions of dollars by promising returns of 50 percent in just forty-five days. The day of reckoning came, as it inevitably does, and as a result, his name is now synonymous with a financial scheme intended to defraud investors.

And speaking of Ponzi schemes, Bernie Madoff "made off" with billions of dollars from supposedly sophisticated investors.

While we're on the subject of recent history, a prince from Nigeria once promised me a hefty fee if I would help him bring millions of dollars into the United States.

If you think no one falls for these scams any longer, think again. The only reason many of these scams are still in circulation is that people continue to take the bait.

The dot-com bubble of the late 1990s arrived as the result of a combination of rapidly increasing stock prices, confidence in future profits, and an abundance of venture capital available for internet-related start-ups. Investors were willing to eschew traditional metrics and pay outrageous prices for stocks with no earnings. Technology was the new darling of Wall Street, but after the technology-laden Nasdaq peaked at 5,133 on March 10, 2000, the ensuing decline was devastating.

Something similar happened less than a decade later. Before 2007, home prices in the United States had not fallen significantly since the Great Depression. Real estate was considered a safe investment by almost everyone, given the ever-growing population, and this belief became the cornerstone of an entire investment philosophy. Mortgage brokers would make loans to anyone who could fog a mirror, assuming rising prices would provide ample collateral in the case of default. Rising prices made even the most reckless real estate endeavors look like brilliance. When real estate prices spiraled downward, the entire financial system collapsed yet again. With the dot-com boom and then the explosion of interest in real estate, we were all told that "this time is different"—and we bought it.

Noted economist Robert Schiller coined the term irrational exuberance, and he posited that it arises as a consequence of human psychology. When a large number of people are generating significant profits from an investment, it seems too good to pass up, so other people feel the need to participate. Those who are still uncertain about their buying decisions subconsciously pacify those fears by convincing their friends to follow suit, even if those hidden doubts were well-founded. There's comfort in crowds. In Schiller's opinion, this explains all investment mania.

People are more gullible than they believe they are. The fear of missing out (FOMO) and looking stupid as a result can be a strong motivator. Trust is often misplaced. If you listen to a speech that strikes you as less than stellar while those around you react with a standing ovation, you might doubt your assessment and will probably stand and applaud as well. Going along with the crowd is the path of least resistance. Manias create bubbles, and bubbles eventually pop. There's a reason for the saying "if it sounds too good to be true, chances are it is."

Bubbles, by their very definition, are next to impossible to predict. That said, what are you supposed to do with this short history lesson to avoid becoming the next victim?

I'm going to make it easy for you. In this book, you will learn how to implement a profitable investment strategy that is not subject to the consequences of groupthink.

How has your FOMO resulted in poor decision-making in the past?

When was the last time you were duped into an investment that sounded too good to be true and came to regret it?

Are you willing to meet the next "sure thing" that comes down the pike with a healthy dose of cynicism?

If an investment sounds too good to be true, run.

CHAPTER 13

BUT IT MUST BE TRUE

> *Believe nothing, O monks, merely because you have been told it . . . or because it is traditional, or because you yourselves have imagined it. Do not believe what your teacher tells you merely out of respect for the teacher. But whatsoever, after due examination and analysis, you find to be conducive to the good, the benefit, the welfare of all beings—that doctrine believe and cling to and take it as your guide.*
>
> —Gautama Buddha

Prevailing wisdom can often lead you astray. "Who the hell wants to hear actors talk?" asked H. M. Warner of Warner Brothers in 1927 at a time when silent movies were all the rage. Oops. In 1977, Ken Olsen, founder of Digital Equipment, said, "There is no reason anyone would want a computer in their home."

These industry leaders missed the mark, revealing that holding onto prevailing wisdom often squelches innovation. Fred Smith, the founder of Federal Express, wrote a paper while at Yale in which he proposed a reliable overnight delivery service. His professor told him that if he wanted better than a C on his essay, his idea must be plausible. Steve Jobs sought early funding from Atari and Hewlett-Packard, and both passed.

But what is the prevailing "wisdom" on personal finance?

Owning your own home is the cornerstone of achieving the American dream. Maybe. Maybe not.

A loss on paper is not a loss until you sell. False, but that advice might make you feel better.

You can't go wrong by taking a profit. Unless, of course, you followed my lead and bought 200 shares of Apple Computer at $22 a share shortly after it went public in 1980 and proceeded to sell it a few days later for an impressive 20 percent gain. Four stock splits and thirty years later, those measly 200 shares, as of January 1, 2020, would have grown to 11,200 shares at $300 a share for a total of $3.36 million.

One of my favorite lines from a recent radio ad claims that gold has always been the best hedge against both *inflation*, a general increase in prices and loss of purchasing power, and *deflation*, a reduction in the general level of prices. I'm still trying to wrap my head around that logic. Just because everyone you know says something is a good idea doesn't necessarily make it so. A healthy dose of skepticism and common sense will serve you well. Question everything, even the words in this book.

Think back to the times in your life when commonly held beliefs proved to be incorrect.

Are you willing to accept that prevailing wisdom is not synonymous with the truth?

Can you make decisions independent from crowd sentiment?

Live in the question
and not in the answer.

CHAPTER 14

THE FALLACY OF SUNK COST

> *The past is a great place, and I don't want to erase it or to regret it, but I don't want to be its prisoner either.*
>
> —Mick Jagger

In economics, the term *sunk cost* refers to any loss that has already been incurred and is now unrecoverable. If you're like most people, you are a frequent victim of the fallacy of sunk cost. Have you ever kept watching a lousy movie or continued reading a bad book because you thought you were too far into it to quit? Did stopping somehow seem like an acknowledgment that you would have wasted time already invested? When dining out, do you feel compelled to clean your plate, even if you're full, because you're going to have to pay for the food regardless? That's sunk-cost thinking, and it's flawed.

Emotional investments of time, money, or other committed resources can easily lead one to fall prey to the sunk cost fallacy. We give the past too much credit when it comes to taking the next step forward. This fallacy encourages behavior that can often lead to irrational decisions that are emotional and imprudent, which can wreak havoc on your investments.

Poker players frequently make foolish calls because of the money they have already committed to the pot rather than calculating whether or not the odds going forward are in their favor. Pros know this and take full advantage of it in their play.

The roulette ball has no memory. To place a significant bet on red after the last five spins landed on black does not improve your odds for the next turn of the wheel landing on red. If I flip a coin and it comes up heads ten times in a row, the next flip is still as likely to land on heads as it is on tails. In the same way, a stock that's doing poorly now doesn't have better odds tomorrow simply because you don't want to take a loss. Merely being aware of the fallacy of sunk cost will help you make more rational decisions. If what you're doing isn't working, I suggest you get up from the table and try something else.

When it comes to making investment decisions, it is imperative to recognize that in the majority of situations, you should ignore *cost basis*—the original value or purchase price of an asset or investment. However, sunk costs can easily make you lose sight of this principle. I have witnessed many poor investment decisions made by otherwise intelligent people because of their unwillingness to pay the taxman.

When deciding on whether to buy more, sell, or hold a stock you currently own, the price you paid should be, in most cases, irrelevant. Your decision should be based primarily on your outlook going forward—whether you think the stock will be valued higher or lower. Whether or not you have a profit or a loss, the advice should be the same. If you're frustrated that you'll be taking a loss by selling, don't let that stop you from selling if the outlook is weak. Chances are you'll be looking at a more significant loss down the road. This concept is extremely challenging for most people to comprehend. It will serve you well in the future in many areas of your life if you can grasp this concept and divorce yourself from the emotion often present in these decisions. It's essential.

Here's a prime example. A friend of mine was trying to decide whether or not she should sell her beach house. It was primarily an income-producing rental with a history of staying booked solid during the summer months. Nonetheless, the bottom line was a paltry return of less than 4 percent annually, and managing it required a significant investment of her time. A hurricane or a slower rental season could quickly turn a small profit into a losing investment. It was, however, worth less than she had paid for it, and the thought of selling it at a loss was unacceptable. I asked her whether she would be willing to purchase the property at the current market value, given her knowledge of the rental history, property taxes, and maintenance required in owning the property (all sunk costs).

"Hell no!" she replied.

So, I told her to sell it. She had the choice of owning the beach house or having the cash. It was emotionally challenging for her to understand my logic, but eventually, she came around and let it go.

When deciding whether to sell a stock, a house, or other investment, ask yourself that question: If you didn't own it, would you buy it now at the current price? If the answer is a resounding no, it just might be time to sell.

When the sunk cost fallacy shows up again in your life (and it will), identify it, put in on the shelf, and do the next right thing without regard to irrelevant history.

Where have sunk costs led to poor decision-making in your life? If you paid good money for a pair of shoes that hurt your feet every time you put them on, why are they still in your closet?

Eliminate sunk costs

from your decision-making process.

CHAPTER 15

ADRENALINE JUNKIES

> *Patience is bitter, but its fruit is sweet.*
>
> —Jean-Jacques Rousseau

Ask any professional poker player to cite the most common mistake made by amateurs, and you will often hear that they play too many hands. Winning poker is a grind. An experienced cash player is often content winning just one or two pots an hour while slowly and methodically building a respectable bankroll. Patience in playing poker is a virtue that pays off over the long term. When the right cards eventually come, and the odds shift from being unfavorable to favorable, the pro will enter the hand, often with a meaningful amount of money. Sometimes it seems like an eternity before a playable hand comes along. Frustration, boredom, and impatience settle in. Before long, the amateur succumbs to the need for action by overplaying a lousy hand, and a downward spiral ensues. It's human nature. We crave excitement.

I have learned this lesson the hard way, as have most accomplished poker players. After two hours of holding no two cards that are remotely related, pocket fives can look like pocket aces, and I've often overplayed my hand to my detriment. If only I had employed a little patience; better cards would have come eventually. This lesson has served me well in poker and other areas of my life.

Poker is a zero-sum game after subtracting the house's cut. In other words, for every dollar made, there is a dollar lost. Countless times, I have sat at relatively low-limit poker tables mainly populated by tourists whose time in town is brief. They crave action and are, more often than not, unwilling to exercise patience and wait for good cards. They overbet weak hands and make ridiculous bluffs. They win a big hand and then lose an even bigger one. They mitigate their losses by rationalizing the "entertainment value" of their experience. These players are mentally prepared to lose, and I have no problem being on the receiving end of their contribution. Business is business. They get a great experience, and I get paid for helping deliver it. Works for me.

What does this have to do with investing? Plenty. Investing should be a grind as well, and sometimes it can be tedious. Prudent investing requires patience. It can be tempting to act hastily to make a quick profit. Don't kid yourself. If you can find a single day trader who has honestly profited over the long haul, then you know one more than I do. They seem to remember their gains clearly, file away their losses, and continue to play what amounts to a losing game—precisely like gamblers. Some, after they lose all their money trading, dare to try to recoup their losses by marketing their "sure thing" trading systems to an uninitiated public. Many gamblers I know claim to have made tons of money over their lifetimes, but somebody out there is keeping the casinos afloat.

Be an investor, not a gambler. You will learn in this book how to succeed over time with your investments. The stock market has experienced incredible long-term growth, and the patient investor will reap the rewards. There will be good markets and bad markets, interest rates will change, and the economy will ebb and flow. Change is a given. Don't forget that when the race was over, the turtle beat the hare.

◆

Do you have a habit of remembering your winnings and forgetting your losses?

Can you approach investing with a calm, clear head and look for excitement elsewhere?

Are you willing to be a boring investor?

If you're craving excitement, channel it into something other than short-term trading.

CHAPTER 16

MINDSET RECAP

" *When our knowing exceeds our sensing, we will no longer be deceived by the illusion of our senses.*

—Walter Russell

We have covered a lot in the preceding pages. I trust that my words struck a chord somewhere along the way and that you've opened your mind to a better idea of how to handle your money. To summarize:

- ♣ Take the necessary time to learn the rules of the game before you play.
- ♣ Become mindful of your relationship with money. Rather than having it be a burden, allow it to become a tool that works for you.
- ♣ A goal unwritten or without a due date is a pipe dream.

♣ Seek clarity, and above all, start being honest with yourself.

♣ If you don't know where you're going, any road will take you there.

♣ Your definition of wealth is yours to make and does not require the approval of others.

♣ Get sticky with your money.

♣ You don't need to earn a pile of money to finance a comfortable retirement. Remember Beans.

♣ Short-term behavior is the breeding ground for long-term consequences—both good and bad.

♣ Beware the penalties of succumbing to the desire for immediate gratification.

♣ Start paying attention to how you spend your money. Invest in appreciating assets instead of things that erode in value.

♣ Denial is insidious, ubiquitous, and counterproductive.

♣ Emotions are your archenemy when it comes to managing your money. When they rear their ugly head (and they will), thank them for sharing, and put them off to the side before making any significant decisions.

♣ If everyone thinks it's a good idea, be cautious and do your homework.

♣ Take prevailing wisdom with a grain of salt. History is replete with stories about how the majority was wrong.

♣ Notice where sunk-cost thinking shows up in your decision-making process.

♣ Patience is a virtue when it comes to investing. Time is your ally.

Revisit this chapter periodically to keep your head on straight.

Now that you have completed a brief course in psychology, it's time to go to school and learn about the various components of the financial landscape—the good, the bad, and the ugly.

The road to financial freedom starts with having the proper mindset.

KNOWLEDGE

CHAPTER 17

ESSE QUAM VIDERI

> " *The way to gain a good reputation is to endeavor to be what you desire to appear.*
>
> —Socrates

I'm a pretty good poker player. I primarily attribute that to paying close attention to the cast of characters at the table and observing how they play the game. Are they on vacation, meaning their potential (and probable) poker losses amount to nothing more than the cost of entertainment? Are they conservative or reckless? Do they have any idea what they're doing? It's essential to know with whom you are doing business.

Should you engage the services of a financial adviser, you will find that many of them proudly display a long string of initials after their names to convince you of their competence and professionalism. What these initials represent can be a mystery to the average investor, and you need to know the landscape you're playing in. Let's look at the four best financial credentials.

CHARTERED FINANCIAL ANALYST (CFA)

CFA is a globally recognized professional designation awarded by the CFA Institute, which requires candidates to complete exams in accounting, economics, ethics, money management, and security analysis. CFA is one of the most respected designations in finance and the gold standard in the field of financial management. It is equivalent to achieving a master's degree in finance, with accompanying minors in accounting, economics, statistical analysis, and portfolio analysis. The majority of individuals who have earned this designation work for banks, hedge funds, pensions, or mutual fund companies.

CERTIFIED FINANCIAL PLANNER (CFP)

CFP is a formal recognition of expertise in financial planning, taxes, insurance, estate planning, and retirement. This designation deserves a certain level of respect, given the rigorous and comprehensive study it requires. The CFP

Board's Code of Ethics and Standards of Conduct requires CFP professionals to uphold the principles of integrity, objectivity, competence, and confidentiality. They make a commitment to put their clients' interests first at all times when providing financial advice.

CHARTERED INSTITUTE OF MANAGEMENT ACCOUN-TANT (CIMA)

The Investments and Wealth Institute issue the CIMA credential. This designation takes close to a year to complete and focuses on portfolio construction.

CERTIFIED PUBLIC ACCOUNTANT (CPA)

You are most certainly aware of this designation. It's focused on taxes and bookkeeping services. Achieving this certification is no walk in the park either.

All of the credentials above have prerequisites and require substantial study time and rigorous testing.

Furthermore, the Financial Industry Regulatory Authority (FINRA) is responsible for administering the coursework and examination for its various licenses, including:

♣ *Series 7.* The gold standard for financial adviser licensees, allowing them to sell almost any financial product, including stocks, bonds, options, and futures. This license does not, however, authorize the trading of commodities, which requires a separate Series 3 license. Series 7 is one of the most challenging and comprehensive licenses for a financial adviser to obtain and should warrant at least a modicum of your respect.

♣ *Series 6.* This allows advisers to sell packaged products such as mutual funds, but not individual stocks and bonds.

♣ *Series 63.* Every state requires this license, which denotes knowledge of pertinent state laws and regulations.

♣ *Series 65.* This is required for financial advisers who are compensated by fees instead of commissions.

An individual who holds one or more of those four licenses is a genuine, credentialed financial adviser. Sadly, the investment landscape is chock-full of people who call themselves financial advisers, making the moniker somewhat misleading. While financial advisers do not technically have to be licensed to offer advice, they are generally required to have various securities licenses to sell financial products. The truth is that anyone can pretty much call themselves a financial adviser these days. The licenses required to conduct business depend on the types of financial products sold and the method of compensation.

Over the past decade or so, an alarming trend has emerged. The life insurance industry has created a host of financial products with underlying performance linked to a specific stock index such as the Standard and Poor (S&P) 500. Life insurance salespeople who possess the life insurance license required to sell these products (not securities) all too often misrepresent themselves as being on an equal footing with an adviser holding a Series 7 license. Considering the training, study, and rigorous testing that is mandatory for individuals who earn one of the investment adviser designations or licenses I just mentioned, you'll quickly see that someone with only an insurance license is not on par with a credentialed, qualified financial adviser. Regulated by entirely separate governing bodies, that person should be more accurately called a life insurance agent.

To further muddy the water, you can find plenty of low-quality designations that are nothing more than marketing ploys designed to convey a level of expertise that is often absent. Many of these designations have few or no prerequisites, entail little or no study, and require no testing. Acquiring many of these designations involves little more than the ability to write a check. The list of dubious certifications is long and ever growing, and it will serve you well to separate the wheat from the chaff.

Beware of individuals with certifications for selling financial products, such as annuities or certifications, that target religious groups and seniors. Sadly, many seniors are particularly vulnerable, often falling prey to an imposed fear of running out of money. Take a close look at certifications that use letters that mirror highly regarded credentials. For example, don't confuse CFPN (Christian Financial Professionals Network) with CFP, the legitimate certification for certified financial planners.

When choosing to work with a financial professional, it's essential you understand how the level of education they have acquired—and their resultant expertise—can be beneficial to your investment needs. If your current or prospective adviser holds one or more designations, ask them to explain what these certifications represent in terms of study, knowledge, and testing. Ask about the conferring organization and whether there are any requirements for continuing education.

Esse quam videri is Latin for "to be rather than to seem." It is also the motto for my home state of North Carolina. Sage advice.

♦

Have you been impressed with an adviser because they possessed a host of letters after their name, even if those letters meant little or nothing to you?

Are you comfortable asking direct questions to your adviser, potential or current, to ascertain their value to you?

Know when to be impressed
and when to chuckle
when you read
a financial adviser's business card.

CHAPTER 18

TALKING HEADS

> *I'd like to be known for more than being the guy in the big suit.*
>
> —David Byrne

A professional poker player once told me the reason for the game's popularity is that most players judge their ability the same way they do their sexual prowess. They all think they're better than average when, in reality, half of them are not.

Most people are primarily self-serving and, for that reason alone, take the advice dispensed by talking heads in the financial world with a grain of salt. It's unfortunate, but some people dispensing financial news and advice aren't as concerned about your economic needs as you might believe. Conflicts of interest are everywhere in the world of finance, and you must recognize them and keep them in a proper perspective.

Financial advisers are often paid commissions for the sale of products that may or may not be in their clients' best interests. The days of stockbrokers charging exorbitant commissions on every trade are all but over. Fee-only advisers—those who are paid by the hour or receive a reasonable percentage of the assets they manage—are a much better alternative.

CNBC, Bloomberg, and other financial media outlets routinely feature so-called experts who work hard at appearing intelligent and crave the spotlight. These individuals are often motivated to raise additional assets to manage or to tout the stocks they own. Everyone has their day in the sun when they look like a genius, and even a broken clock is right twice a day. The media turns its focus to the pundits who just so happened to be correct in their assessment at a particular moment of time—Monday-morning quarterbacks, I call them. During a *Goldilocks economy* (one that maintains steady growth without too much inflation), the stock market tends to perform well, ushering in the perpetual bulls who are right—until they aren't. Then come the doom-and-gloomers who crawl out of their caves during market selloffs and pontificate on their uncanny foresight. Of course, they forget to mention the fact that they were sitting on the sidelines during the previous bull market, waiving at the passersby. And so it goes.

The financial news media wants the market to go up. Bull markets are good for business because when people are interested in stocks, ratings are higher. This inherent bias toward bullishness is pervasive on Wall Street.

If you stay glued to the financial media, moving money from one idea to another based on what some "expert" has to say on any given day, that will not help you accumulate wealth and achieve your financial goals. It is a time-consuming, inefficient way to manage your money.

Markets ebb and flow. Business cycles go through phases of expansion and contraction. If a Democrat is in the Oval Office during periods of rising markets, he will pat himself on the back and take full credit. The previous Republican president will claim that what you are seeing is the result of the seeds they planted during their prior reign.

I believe both are wrong and that business cycles, for the most part, are bigger and more powerful than politicians are willing to admit. Anyway, that's what my economics professor at Duke told us in class.

Financial media certainly has its place when it comes to disseminating essential news developments. Still, it primarily serves as a twenty-four-seven for-profit source of entertainment for those of you who enjoy that stuff. Viewership sells ads. Even the Weather Channel has become an entertainment medium. Having lived in the hurricane "cone of death" on the North Carolina coast for over twenty years, I have seen my share of "killer storms" that failed to knock down a single tree, and mere "bad" ones that caused extensive damage. But no matter the storm, we all tune in to enjoy the suspense. We love noise.

Take the time necessary to examine the motives of the talking heads you see on TV as well as the adviser sitting across the table from you. Watching the financial news around the clock can lead you to second-guess your existing holdings and implement unnecessary changes. Try on a little cynicism. The more you handle a bar of soap, the smaller it gets. Think of your capital as that bar of soap, and imagine the sliver you'll be left with if you play around with it too much.

♦

Have you ever felt that a recommendation you were given was in the best interest of the one dispensing it rather than you?

What poor investment decisions have you made the past because you paid attention to and reacted to the noise?

Where does noise show up in your life today, and what steps can you make to ignore it?

If you can learn to remain stoic,
market volatility
can work for you instead of against you.

CHAPTER 19

THE RAKE

> *It's not what you pay a man, but what he costs you that counts.*
>
> —Will Rogers

Casinos can splurge on opulent decor, offer free drinks, and still make a profit because the games they offer have a predictable and quantifiable edge over the player. The number of customers who walk through their doors directly correlates with profitability. The predictability that comes from the *law of large numbers*—a statistical term stating that the larger a sample size grows, the more predictable the outcome—takes care of the rest. Despite what your uncle Ernie told you about his last big win in Las Vegas, house games, including blackjack, roulette, and baccarat, are unbeatable in the long run.

Poker is different from other gambling games in that it pits you against other players rather than the house. How do casinos make money on poker games? The dealers take a *rake,* typically a percentage of the pot—say, 10 percent— with a cap. As money moves from player to player, the house methodically siphons off the appropriate amount of chips from every pot. A fast table can accommodate as many as thirty-five hands an hour. If the average rake is $10, that table will earn $350 an hour for the house. It doesn't matter to the casino which players win or lose—their revenue is predictable.

Inexperienced players rarely notice the rake, much less quantify it. Although poker, unlike other casino games, includes a significant element of skill, the rake is a real headwind that, while not insurmountable, must be overcome.

The investment world has its rake as well. In considering your investments, you should be clear on what you are spending and what you are receiving in return. While there are many low-cost investment options available in the marketplace, there is more to wealth building than focusing on price. It's easy to be penny-wise and pound-foolish.

I know many advisers who charge big bucks because their experience and expertise make their counsel invaluable. On the other hand, there are also those whose counsel is dubious despite the hefty fees and commissions they charge for doing what you could easily do on your own.

If you are comfortable being a do-it-yourself (DIY) investor, then, by all means, look to low-cost investment vehicles to implement your wealth-building strategies. If you are like most people and feel you need some guidance, insist on complete transparency regarding fees, and make sure that the service and performance received is worth the price you pay.

There is nothing wrong with an investment adviser charging a fee. That is their job, and they are entitled to making a living. If you haven't done so in the past, begin to pay closer attention to any commissions or fees involved, because they will affect your portfolio's performance.

There are many investments structured to appear as though there are no costs to the investor, which constitutes a gross misrepresentation of the facts. This deception frequently occurs in the sale of certain insurance investments, mutual funds, and illiquid products with hefty *surrender charges*. These are additional charges you must pay if you withdraw money before a contractual number of years has elapsed. If the adviser is earning a commission, the client is paying it somewhere. Often this information is deeply embedded in the fine print. Regardless of the obscurity, an adviser who is a fiduciary is required to disclose how their compensation is derived. Ask.

When describing a particular investment or packaged product to a prospective buyer, advisers all too often point out the "fact" that there is no commission whatsoever charged to the client. There is sleight of hand at work here. The adviser typically gets paid upfront by the company that sponsored the product. In short, there's no such thing as a free lunch. Even if there's "no commission," you're still paying dearly, and it's seldom necessary to own a product priced in this manner.

After you have read this book in its entirety, you will have at your fingertips everything you need to bid farewell to unnecessary commissions and fees. Pennies add up to dollars. For example, $100,000 accumulating at an average annual return of 8 percent grows to $1,093,573 in thirty years. If you subtract a 1 percent annual management fee, your investment would have realized an annualized return of 7 percent and grown to only $811,650! Is it worth an extra $281,923 to you learn how to manage your money on your own and dispense with paying high fees? It certainly is to me. Business is business. Keep reading, and I will show you how to perform even better.

If you have a current adviser, how much are you paying for that privilege?

What are you receiving in return?

Are you willing to learn how to do it on your own?

Reducing what appear to be modest expenses will add up to significant dollars over time.

TWENTY QUESTIONS

> *He who asks a question remains a fool for five minutes;*
> *he who does not ask a question remains a fool forever.*
>
> —Chinese proverb

People typically spend more time planning their vacation than they do planning for their retirement. If you are considering working with a financial adviser, I strongly suggest that you ask a lot of questions before committing yourself. Or perhaps it's time to reevaluate your current one.

Financial "experts" reside on every corner these days, and they all have impressive titles like estate planner or investment counselor. In my experience, only a handful of them has the requisite knowledge and expertise required to help preserve and grow your financial assets.

Never hesitate to interview a prospective adviser. Answers to the following questions will go a long toward developing a professional relationship that can go the distance.

- ♣ What formal education have you received?
- ♣ How long have you been in the business of providing financial advice?
- ♣ Are you independent or employed by a firm?
- ♣ Do you have an investment philosophy, and if so, what is it?
- ♣ How are you compensated?
- ♣ What investment products, if any, do you employ?
- ♣ Can you describe your typical client's stage of life and their investment goals?
- ♣ What licenses and designations do you hold?
- ♣ Do you provide financial planning, and, if so, is there a fee for that service?
- ♣ How often do you typically meet with your clients?
- ♣ What performance reporting, if any, do you provide?
- ♣ What strategies do you employ during a bull market?
- ♣ What strategies do you employ during a bear market?
- ♣ Do you insist on trading *discretion*—making trades in customer accounts without first consulting the customer?

- ♣ How do you research your investment ideas?

- ♣ What do you consider to be a good return?

- ♣ How long do you intend to stay in this business?

- ♣ What contingency plans, if any, do you have in place should something happen to you?

- ♣ What added value do you bring to justify your fees?

- ♣ Would you provide me with contact information for three clients whose investment objectives are similar to mine who have been with you for at least five years?

Should you decide to engage the services of a financial adviser, I recommend you sit down with that person and ask these questions. Don't email your questions first and allow the adviser time to prepare answers. Catch them off guard and see how they respond. I have heard many humorous stories of advisers looking like deer in headlights when confronted by a potential client with this list of questions. If the adviser starts to squirm in their chair or gives you vague and unsatisfactory answers, thank them for their time and move on to the next person on your list of potential advisers.

◆

Are you willing to ask these questions?

If so, won't it feel better knowing you did your homework?

If you're going to engage

the services of a financial adviser,

make sure all your questions

are answered to your complete satisfaction

before you proceed.

CHAPTER 21

WHAT IS STOCK ANYWAY?

" *Investing should be more like watching paint dry or watching grass grow. If you want excitement, take $800, and go to Las Vegas.*

—Paul Samuelson

Stock—also referred to as *shares* or *equity*—is a type of security representing proportional ownership in the issuing company. It entitles its holder to their share of dividends paid and price appreciation if any occurs. You should be allocating a significant portion of your investable assets to the stock market to participate in the growth of companies. There are mainly two types of stock—common and preferred.

Common stock is, well, common. When people are talking about stocks in general, this is the type of investment they are referring to. Over time, common stocks have out-performed almost every other investment vehicle. It is essential to understand that higher returns nearly always correlate with higher volatility. Markets are cyclical, meaning they experience periods of both rising and falling prices. For investors to enjoy the long-term potential of investing in stocks, they must be willing to accept a certain degree of price fluctuation.

Preferred stock is a hybrid type of investment possessing both bond (see the following chapter) and stock characteristics. It's safer than common stock and somewhat riskier than bonds. The dividend is more secure and predictable than common stock dividends, and depending on the type of preferred stock, there is a possibility for appreciation. In my ongoing effort to make the investing process as simple for you as possible, I will confine all further discussion to common stocks.

The long-term trend in the stock market is an upward one, and with the right strategy in place, participation in this growth can produce significant wealth over time. Yes, there will be times when markets perform poorly and test your resolve, but historically these are short-term speed bumps followed by an upward surge to new highs.

Stocks trade on *stock exchanges*, which can be physical or virtual. The three primary exchanges in the United States are the New York Stock Exchange (NYSE), the National Association of Securities Dealers Automated Quotation System (NASDAQ), and the American Stock Exchange (ASE). If you buy individual stocks, your transactions will likely occur on one of these exchanges.

There are many ways to categorize stocks. Some of the more common classifications are growth, value, large-cap, mid-cap, small-cap, domestic, international, and emerging markets. There are eleven major sectors that more precisely define stocks, including the consumer discretionary, consumer staples, energy, financials, health care, industrials, materials, real estate, technology, and telecom sectors. Every one of these sectors has enjoyed their day in the sun when they outperformed all the others. Knowing which one will shine tomorrow is next to impossible. The prudent investor spreads his bets out across the board, never putting too many eggs in a single basket.

There are three simple ways to invest in equities:

- ♣ *Individual stocks.* This is when you buy stock in a company such as Amazon.

- ♣ *Mutual funds.* These professionally managed pools invest in a large number of stocks and provide the necessary diversification with even the smallest of investment dollars.

- ♣ *Exchange-traded funds (ETFs).* These are similar in composition to mutual funds but trade on stock exchanges like individual stocks.

What's the most intelligent way to participate in stocks? Individual stocks have more cachet, especially if you believe Uncle Louie's delusion that he knows something nobody else knows. Achieving diversification is inherently difficult without massive amounts of money, and even then, it's typically hard to make a strong case for purchasing individual stocks. Mutual funds and ETFs provide broad, diversified exposure to an index such as the S&P 500, a specific country or region, or a particular niche, and you don't have to buy hundreds of individual stocks to achieve diversification. There are distinct differences between the two as well. Mutual funds typically price once a day at market close (4:00 p.m. ET), and ETFs can be bought or sold during regular market hours (9:30 a.m. ET to 4:00 p.m. ET).

Mutual funds and ETFs are either *passive* or *actively managed*. The objective of a passive fund, or *index fund,* is to mirror the performance of an underlying index, such as the Dow Jones Industrial Average. In contrast, actively managed funds allow the fund manager to trade the portfolio to outperform the respective benchmark. Collectively, passive funds have had the upper hand in performance over the long haul, chiefly due to lower trading costs and management expenses.

ETFs and index mutual funds are more tax efficient than actively managed mutual funds. Many ETFs are thinly traded, resulting in large spreads between the bid and ask prices, making trading costly. If you're going the ETF route, stay with ETFs that trade a large volume of shares to ensure liquidity.

Unlike mutual funds, market forces determine ETF prices. As a result, ETFs often trade at a premium or a discount to the value of the underlying portfolio. This characteristic can prove advantageous to the ETF investor investing systematically. More on this later.

Of the three essential avenues for investing in stocks, I prefer passive ETFs, and you should find comfort in these as well.

◆

Have you ever bought an individual stock only to see its value plummet?

What does diversification mean to you?

Simplify by confining your stock investments to passive ETFs.

CHAPTER 22

THE NAME IS BOND

 *An investment in knowledge pays the best interest.*

—Benjamin Franklin

The average investor often misunderstands bonds. At a glance, they appear somewhat pedestrian, but they can be rather complicated investment vehicles. Stocks and bonds are both *securities*—fungible, negotiable financial instruments that represent some type of monetary value—and that's about all they have in common. While stock ownership represents an equity position in the issuing company, bondholders are lenders. A bondholder has a creditor's stake in the issuing entity.

A *fixed-rate bond* pays the same amount of interest, usually semiannually, from the date of issue until the maturity date. As long as the bond issuer does not default, the bondholder can accurately predict what the return on investment will be if the bond is held until the end of its term, otherwise known as reaching *maturity*.

The main risk in owning fixed-rate bonds is changing interest rates. Fixed-rate bond prices fluctuate in value, moving in the opposite direction of interest rates. How much do bond prices move? That's a difficult question to answer with high precision. It depends on *duration*—an approximate measure of a bond or bond fund's sensitivity to changes in interest rates. The duration for the Barclays US Aggregate Bond Index, the broadest benchmark for the bond market, is 5.65 years as I am writing this sentence. Thus, if interest rates were to rise by one percentage point, the Barclays Aggregate would fall in price by approximately 5.65 percent; a half-point decrease in interest rates would cause an increase in the value of the bond by roughly 2.83 percent, and so on.

Typically, fixed-rate bonds with longer maturities pay higher interest. They also have a higher duration and are thus more susceptible to fluctuating interest rates. Fixed-rate bonds are also rated based on their perceived safety. The higher the safety rating, the lower the yield. It's risk versus reward.

If your crystal ball tells you that interest rates are going to fall, bonds would probably be a good bet. You would be locking in a higher interest rate than would be available later, and the value of your bond will appreciate. However, should interest rates rise, you would be receiving less interest than the prevailing rates offer, causing your bonds to decline in value.

To get a higher yield, investors all too often jump into bonds and other income-producing instruments without fully understanding the risks involved. *Savings accounts* and *money market funds* are short-term investments with little to no risk and do not share the interest-rate risk inherent in the fixed-rate bond market. Fixed-rate bonds certainly have a place in more balanced portfolios with shorter time horizons. Just like stocks, bonds can be purchased individually through a mutual fund or an ETF. My advice, again, is to stay with ETFs.

As you near or enter retirement, you should increase your bond allocation to lessen the volatility of your portfolio. Diversifying among different maturities within your bond allocation makes sense as well. With shorter life expectancies come shorter time horizons, and prudence dictates that you should allocate prudently to mitigate the overall risk.

◆

Do you understand the inverse relationship between interest rates and bond values?

Can you see the advantages of including bonds in your portfolio?

Slowly increase your bond exposure as you near or enter your retirement years.

CHAPTER 23

A CRASH COURSE ON RETIREMENT ACCOUNTS

> *My interest is in the future because I am going to spend the rest of my life there.*
>
> —Charles Kettering

You should direct a significant portion of your investments into retirement accounts. Many companies offer such accounts to their employees, including, but not limited to, defined benefit plans and defined contribution plans.

Defined benefit plans, often referred to as *pensions plans*, seem to be disappearing as a corporate benefit, remaining only with federal, state, and local government entities. These public pension plans, funded by the employer, provide an income benefit based on years of service and average salary. If you are the recipient of such a pension, consider yourself fortunate. This income can go a long way toward meeting your retirement income needs without requiring contributions from you along the way. One caveat here worth mentioning is that many government-defined benefit plans are severely underfunded, and what may seem to be a certainty at present may not bear the fruit it was intended to provide.

Defined contribution plans are the most common types of plans offered in the workplace. Primarily funded by the employer, they include the 401(k), 403(b), and others. A 401(k) plan is offered by private, for-profit companies, whereas a 403(b) plan is only available to nonprofit organizations and government employees. Established by the employer, these plans allow employees to contribute (hence the term *defined contribution*) via payroll deduction.

Many companies offer a *match*—a percentage added to the employees' retirement accounts from the company coffers based on the level of employee contribution. For example, a company may contribute fifty cents for each dollar of the first 6 percent of income added by the employee. Often there is a *vesting period*—the time required for an employee to own the retirement plan contribution made on his behalf by the company—established to reward the tenure of an employee. For example, there may be a five-year vesting period stipulating that 20 percent of the employer's contributions become the property of the employee each year until they become fully vested. Receiving a match is essentially free money, and it should be abundantly clear that you should use your income to take full advantage of the match available. As of 2020, the maximum amount an employee can contribute is $19,500 for both the 401(k) and 403(b).

Contributions to both the 401(k) and 403(b) may be available on either a pre-tax or after-tax basis. If contributions are made pre-tax, the income is tax deferred until withdrawal. Conversely, after-tax contributions are tax-free upon withdrawal. The IRS is going to get paid either today or tomorrow. Should you take withdrawals before age fifty-nine and a half, there is an early withdrawal penalty of 10 percent. There are some exceptions to this penalty for certain educational and medical expenses, however.

If you are self-employed, there are several options available:

♣ *SEP-IRAs* are for self-employed people with one or more employees.

♣ *Solo 401(k)s* and solo *Roth 401(k)s* are for self-employed people with no employees other than a spouse.

♣ *Simple IRAs* are for self-employed people and businesses with up to 100 employees.

Lastly, there are individual retirement plan options available, including:

♣ *Traditional IRAs.* Contributions to traditional IRAs are tax deductible; the income is tax deferred until withdrawal. The annual contribution limit for 2020 is $6,000, or $7,000 if you are fifty years of age or older. Furthermore, your contributions cannot exceed your earnings during the year that you contribute.

♣ *Roth IRAs.* Contributions to Roth IRAs are after-tax, and the income is tax-free. Roth IRAs have the same contribution limits as traditional IRAs, with additional income restrictions.

♣ *Spousal IRAs.* These IRAs can be either traditional or Roth, and they allow a spouse who doesn't work to participate in tax-advantaged savings.

This chapter on retirement accounts may be the shortest one ever written. There have been entire books written on the intricacies of retirement plans. Specific rules and parameters are complex and fluid. By the time you read this, many of the details I highlight here may be obsolete. The bottom line is that for almost every situation, there is a retirement vehicle that will allow a wage earner to sock away money, pre-tax or after-tax, to prepare for their golden years.

◆

Are you eligible for a company retirement plan?

Are you regularly contributing to some type of retirement vehicle?

Can you forgo some degree of immediate gratification to retire with dignity?

Take full advantage of retirement plans that are available for your situation.

CHAPTER 24

THE CONFUSING WORLD OF ANNUITIES

" *Truth is ever to be found in simplicity, and not in the multiplicity and confusion of things.*

—Isaac Newton

Craps is a fast-paced, exciting, and popular table game found in most casinos. In it, players make wagers on the outcome of a roll, or series of rolls, of a pair of dice. It can be an intimidating game for the beginner, as the table seems to have as many as a hundred different kinds of bets available. Some wagers have better odds than others—including Pass or Don't Pass, Come or Don't Come. Staying with these bets gives the house about a 1.4 percent edge—not too shabby in the casino world. If you lay or take odds, this reduces the house edge even further. The other multitude of bets offer significantly poorer odds, and you should avoid making them. So, in essence, what at first glance appears to be overwhelming and endlessly confusing can be distilled down to what amounts to a relatively simple game.

The more difficult an investment is to understand fully, the more cautious you should be. An *annuity*—a contract between you and an insurance company in which you invest either a lump sum or a series of payments in exchange for regular income disbursements, beginning either immediately or down the road—is one such animal. You are probably confused already.

During the *accumulation phase*, the owner makes one or more purchase payments. How that money is invested is determined by the type of annuity you own. The assets grow tax deferred, which is almost invariably beneficial. The *payout phase*—when the owner withdraws income— offers several options for receiving that income, including a lifetime of guaranteed payments or over a specified period. The payout option does not have to be elected until the time comes to begin withdrawals.

Also, annuities offer a *guaranteed death benefit*, a feature that ensures that the beneficiary (as named in the contract) will receive a death benefit should the *annuitant*—the person designated to receive the income—die before the annuity begins paying benefits.

There are essentially two types of annuities—fixed and variable.

Fixed annuities pay guaranteed rates of interest that are typically higher than what you might receive at your bank, and the owner can defer the income to a later date or begin to draw it immediately. Insurance agents can sell this investment product without having a securities license.

Variable annuities provide tax deferral as well and offer investment choices among a select group of subaccounts (think mutual funds) comprised of stock, bond, and money market funds. The performance of the underlying subaccounts determines the performance. A securities license is required to sell this type of annuity.

In theory, annuities make a lot of sense, but they are costly thanks to absurdly high commission structures, penalties for early withdrawals (surrender charges), mortality and expense fees, and income-tax implications. The commissions paid are substantial and are usually omitted or downplayed by the salesperson, who may even go so far as to claim that there is no cost to the buyer. The company is picking up the tab—like the "free lunches" that are anything but free. Insurance companies are not charities, nor should they be. Still, annuities are so convoluted in their design that the average buyer is often at a loss as to what he's buying, leaving him at the mercy of the salesperson, who only conveys what is necessary to complete the sale.

Furthermore, annuities are predominantly illiquid investments, meaning that you can't withdraw money in the early years without coughing up surrender penalties. The bigger the commission, the more extended and punitive the surrender schedules. *Mortality expense charges*—fees charged by the insurance company to cover any losses incurred from a premature death of the insured person—typically hover around the 1.5 to 2 percent range, and the management expenses of the subaccounts can tack on an additional 1 percent. These fees directly affect bottom–line performance. Lastly, annuity income cannot qualify for long-term capital gains treatment, resulting in higher tax rates.

Annuities frequently include an assortment of riders that are difficult to value, such as a guaranteed income, regardless of the underlying performance. These riders only add to the attraction, complexity, and confusion, especially with hidden costs that are quite different from how they appear on the surface.

The biggest problem with annuities is the cost. As the investing public grows in their knowledge and awareness, the competition is beginning to heat up in the insurance industry, inevitably forcing companies to revamp their product lines by reducing their costs dramatically. Some already have. If they don't adjust, annuity sales will surely plummet. There are exceptions to every rule, but until the expenses associated with owning an annuity come down to Earth, there are more cost-effective alternatives for your hard-earned money.

If you own an annuity, do you truly know what you own and why?

Do yourself a favor and just say no to annuities.

CHAPTER 25

SMOKE AND MIRRORS

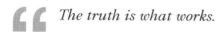 *The truth is what works.*

—William James

There's one more annuity out there that deserves a chapter all its own.

Perhaps you have received an invitation to attend a presentation at a local steakhouse. The mailer you received promised that you'd "learn" how to make money when the stock market goes up and lose nothing when the stock market goes down. It sounds like a great deal, doesn't it? Why would you not put all your money into something like that? It's the best of both worlds! Well, as they say, if it seems too good to be true, it probably is. Take heed. There is much more to this investment than meets the eye.

What I'm talking about here is the *equity-indexed annuity (EIA)*—a type of annuity promulgated widely by insurance agents who, often purporting themselves to be financial advisers, make presentations laden with half-truths and projections that will never come to fruition. EIA sales have ballooned over the past two decades as an unsuspecting and uneducated public continues throwing money into what they consider the holy grail of investments.

I was hungry and in the mood for a steak one night, so at the last minute, I decided to accept the kind invitation to eat for free with no obligation. Although I was told that the seating was "limited," they were somehow able to squeeze me in. In short, I was horrified not only by the nonsense being presented but also by the number of heads nodding with approval. We were told to expect an average annual return of 8 percent, or thereabouts, on our invested dollars with no risk. This proposition is deceptive and misleading. There was outright giddiness among the attendees as they discovered the answer to all of their investment needs—a real no-brainer. Fortunately, I was able to slip out unnoticed at the conclusion. The steak was excellent, by the way, and I went straight home and took a long shower.

The all-so-trendy EIAs may appear straightforward, but in reality, they are quite complicated. With my education and years of experience, I can unravel and understand some of the most complex financial instruments and make sense of them. I applied my expertise to evaluating the EIA, but under each convoluted layer was yet another. After exhaustive number-crunching, I concluded that these products *might* earn a tad more than inflation, say 3 to 4 percent, but the internal fees could easily bring that number down below 2 percent. That's unacceptable.

But it gets worse.

Commissions paid to the selling agent can be as high as 10 percent, and regardless of what they may have told you, you will pay that commission. Even if you pore over the documentation, the average investor will be hard-pressed, as I was, to discern the fine print. There are ongoing fees withdrawn to generate profit for the insurance company. As for having access to your money, good luck with that. EIA contracts typically allow free withdrawals of 10 percent of the account value, with a cap, every policy year. Should the investor need more, there will be absurdly expensive charges assessed during the so-called surrender period, which can be as long as twenty years.

Insurance companies are not charitable organizations. If you think about it, they seem to own the tallest building in every city, built on the backs of an all-too-eager and unwary public. I often wonder whether the sellers of EIAs are drinking their own Kool-Aid, becoming every bit as duped as the prey they are stalking. Perhaps they believe that they are genuinely doing their clients a favor. I would like to think so. Many of them seem to be such lovely people.

With all the current emphasis on better regulation of the financial services industry, including the new Department of Labor Fiduciary Rule, many insurance agents deserve to be restrained but have thus far gone unchecked. With all the discussions about eliminating excessive and undisclosed fees, there has been little or no progress concerning EIAs. The insurance lobby must be flexing its muscles.

In summary, the equity-indexed annuity is the most fee-burdened investment product that I have seen in my career, making it mathematically impossible to deliver the net return projected. There is only so much money to go around. I would never advise clients to include an EIA in their investment portfolio.

Do you own an equity-indexed annuity?

Have you received your invitation to a free steak dinner?

You will save yourself a lot of money

if you cook your steak at home.

CHAPTER 26

AVOIDING BAD BETS

> *One does not accumulate but eliminate. It is not daily increase but daily decrease. The height of cultivation always runs to simplicity.*
>
> —Bruce Lee

Walk into any casino in the world, and you will find a multitude of games to play. It can be overwhelming for first-time visitors. If gambling fever is grabbing you by the shirttail, I suggest you stick with the games that offer the best odds and ignore the rest.

The worst bets in the casino include blackjack insurance, craps prop bets, keno, and of course, slot machines. Lotteries, while fun to play every once in a blue moon, have abysmal odds. I'm not a fan of lotteries because they tend to separate the poor from what little money they have. It's, in essence, a tax on those who can least afford to pay it.

I prefer poker, as it is the only casino game that pits you against other players and not the house. Also, there are a lot of terrible poker players (affectionally known as *fish*) who seem determined to lose their money, and I welcome their play. Poker requires a certain level of skill, sharpened over years of experience. If you want to learn to play poker, begin with home games among friends and then graduate to the lower-level tables in the casino. If you get too far ahead of yourself by playing at the higher-level tables too soon, I hope you end up playing at mine.

Like a trip to the casino, the road to financial success is full of enticing diversions that lead to nothing but dead ends threatening to upend even the most well-intentioned journey. It is best to avoid these hazards if you want to succeed financially.

While none of us come close to making the right decisions all the time, the process of determining where to invest your money involves, or should involve, an attempt to avoid poor choices and flawed thinking that can cost you dearly. Just as choosing the wrong partner to marry can have lasting consequences, opting for the wrong investment can have severely detrimental effects on your financial well-being. Leaving one company to join another can seem foolish in retrospect. You won't always spot the wolf in sheep's clothing when you make a decision, but you should make every effort to avoid making investment choices that can wreak havoc on your finances for years to come. Caveat emptor. Let the buyer beware.

Bad bets in the world of investing are too numerous to list here. Some involve specific investments, and many are simply the results of unsound thinking. The following list highlights a handful of bad bets you should avoid, all of which I have observed bright people make (and I have certainly made my share):

♣ *Paying high fees.* Unnecessary.

♣ *Having unrealistic expectations.* Keep it real.

♣ *Failing to diversify.* Should be obvious to even the most inexperienced.

♣ *Not taking advantage of pre-tax investments.* More on this later.

♣ *Falling in love with a stock.* I'm not sure this is even legal. Shouldn't be.

♣ *Chasing performance.* Like driving while looking in your rearview mirror.

♣ *Taking too much or too little risk.* Know what you're investing in and why.

♣ *Day trading.* Good luck with that.

♣ *Trading options, futures, and commodities.* Risky and short-term investments are better left to professionals and not worthy of further discussion here.

♣ *Buying "hot tips" from Uncle Louie.* Just don't.

♣ *Buying on margin.* It's rarely advisable to borrow money to buy stocks.

♣ *Chasing yield.* If an investment is paying an unusually high return, there's reason for it that should warrant concern.

♣ *Buying illiquid financial products.* Again, not necessary.

♣ *Buying promissory notes.* If an adviser offers you such an investment, politely decline and promptly contact your state attorney general's office.

♣ *Ignoring the effects of inflation.* Real return, net of inflation, is what truly matters.

♣ *Buying depreciating assets instead of appreciating assets.* Duh!

"Keep it simple, stupid," or KISS, is a design principle the US Navy adopted in 1960. It reflects the belief that most systems work best if kept simple instead of made complicated. This concept undoubtedly applies to the world of personal finance. If you are serious about achieving your financial goals, keeping things simple will significantly enhance the likelihood of your success.

Part of the process involves discarding the bad bets and adopting the good ones, just like you would with habits. The world is a lot more complicated than it used to be. An uncomplicated financial regimen devoid of bad bets will go a long way toward making your life more enjoyable and less stressful. Do yourself a favor and confine your investing in the vehicles and strategies outlined in this book.

◆

Do you have a history of making bad bets?

If so, why did you make them?

Will you commit, to the best of your ability, not to repeat them?

Do you desire simplicity?

Investing does not need to be, nor should be, complicated.

CHAPTER 27

LOOK BEFORE YOU LEAP

> " *Nothing is more disgusting than the majority: because it consists of a few powerful predecessors, of rogues who adapt themselves, of weak who assimilate themselves, and the masses who imitate without knowing at all what they want.*

—Johann Wolfgang von Goethe

Owning a home is generally accepted as being more financially sensible than renting. It's the cornerstone of the American dream, and as is often said, continuing to throw money away to pay rent is a fool's game. There are indeed plenty of benefits to homeownership. For one, your home belongs to you (and also the bank if you have a mortgage), and you're not subject to the whims of a landlord. If you have a fixed-rate mortgage, your payments will remain stable, and the interest on your mortgage is tax deductible. The value of your home may rise with time, and you'll build up equity. The vast majority of people will insist that buying a home as soon as possible is the first step in accumulating wealth. But not so fast. If you dig deeper and compare the real cost of owning a home with renting one, you might be surprised by what you uncover.

In 2007, we witnessed the worst housing market crash in American history. At its core was the unshakable belief that real estate prices always appreciate. Much like how a bull market can make any moron look like a genius, continually rising real estate prices made owning a home the most profitable game in town. Speculation and overleveraging were rampant. Eventually, the smoke cleared, the mirrors shattered, and people realized the truth. In the decade leading up to the 2007 real estate crash, it was immensely profitable to own as much house as you could afford, even if you couldn't afford to furnish it. Fueled by a massive drop in interest rates, prices were skyrocketing, more than offsetting the expenses of owning a home. The tide quickly turned, though, reversing the fortunes of those who had ridden the wave to the crest. If only they had cashed in their chips in 2006 and rented for a few years. Oh, the benefits of hindsight.

Will real estate soar again from current prices, making homeownership a must yet again? I will let you be the judge. As of late 2019, the Case Shiller Home Price Index had climbed to around 220, indicating that home prices, adjusted for inflation, are significantly overvalued compared to a historic mean of 145. Perhaps prices will continue to increase (my crystal ball is a bit dusty), but to make a home purchase with that assumption going forward may be a risky proposition.

But what about the income tax deduction for home mortgage interest? This deduction is wildly popular with homeowners and a perennial hot potato for lawmakers. It goes a long way toward convincing first-time homebuyers that, if they can scrape together enough money for a down payment, they would be foolish to continue renting. With recent tax changes in tax law, many homeowners lost most, if not all, the tax benefits they were receiving as homeowners. Part of the Tax Cuts and Jobs Act (TCJA) all but doubled the standard deduction beginning in 2018. While this tax change raised the income threshold for having to pay any taxes, it also diminished or eliminated the benefit of itemized deductions, which includes mortgage interest. Property taxes are tax-deductible as well, but they are nonetheless an expense, and the tax deductibility may no longer be applicable for the same reason as mortgage interest. More than likely, homeowners have no idea.

Thus, tax savings should no longer be a factor in your decision to purchase a home.

Another factor to consider is the upkeep cost of homeownership. The expense of repairs and maintenance is on the homeowner, not the renter. Life changes like a job transfer, divorce, or growing family could necessitate selling the home, and moving generates another set of costs. Renters, on the other hand, enjoy increased mobility. When change happens, they can be flexible and nimble, allowing them to more easily chase life's next adventure when it unfolds.

Am I suggesting that buying a home should be taken off the table? No, but owning a house is a long-term commitment of time and money, including fixed expenses such as mortgage payments, property taxes, utilities, and insurance. I believe that redirecting those dollars to max-imize your retirement plan contributions and building up your emergency savings fund should be more of a priority in your early years (more on this later).

What about employing your excess cash to purchase income-producing real estate? Although there is often the lack of guaranteed income and inherent illiquidity, this can still be a decent option, provided there is a good reason to expect appreciation. Diversification is a challenge, given the size of the investment typically required. There are many exceptions to this, including buying at distressed prices during periods of declining real estate values.

A fellow poker player from my neighborhood game began flipping real estate at the beach in North Carolina as a side hobby, and between 2002 and 2007, he grew his net worth from virtually zero to over $12 million. I was kicking myself for not having participated personally and banking some easy money, but I just couldn't fathom real estate prices continuing to soar the way they had. I asked him if he had an exit strategy. How much was enough? When are you going to cash in your chips and call it a day? He looked at me with these wild eyes like I was out of my mind and essentially accused me of being an idiot for not jumping into the fray. Within a year, he was bankrupt.

Think long and hard before you leap into homeownership. Thoroughly assess the pros and cons. Ignore groupthink. Renting or owning a smaller home may well be a more prudent move while you are in the process of building wealth.

◆

Have you calculated the actual cost of homeownership, including the tax benefits?

Are you willing to forgo homeownership until you have met other investment goals?

Will you reframe homeownership as a luxury rather than an investment?

Renting or owning a smaller home can be an excellent catalyst for building a hefty portfolio.

CHAPTER 28

IN THE UNLIKELY EVENT

" *Everybody has a plan until they get punched in the mouth.*

—Mike Tyson

Insurance is a great tool, and if used correctly, it can protect you if something unforeseen happens. It would be reckless to ignore the benefits insurance can provide you, but purchasing insurance without careful consideration is foolhardy. Don't be without it, but don't overpay for it or buy coverage you don't need. Somewhere in the middle of these two extremes is a sweet spot that makes sense. Let's look at a few different kinds of insurance.

LIFE INSURANCE

Life insurance provides financial protection to the surviving beneficiaries following the death of the insured. Would there be a money problem if someone in your family died before their time? If the answer is yes, life insurance is needed to replace that asset. In the section on execution, I will cover the right type of life insurance to buy and take you through the calculations to determine the appropriate death benefit.

DISABILITY INSURANCE

These policies provide income if a worker cannot perform their work and earn money as a result of a disability. Many employers include disability insurance as an employee benefit, and if not, it can be purchased individually. It is available in both short-term (typically three to six months) and long-term (for periods longer than six months) packages.

If you are consistently saving money, you should not need short-term disability insurance. If funds permit, purchasing a long-term disability insurance policy should be considered.

HEALTH INSURANCE

Health insurance is an ongoing conundrum, as the political environment surrounding it is changing all the time. If your employer does not offer health insurance as a benefit, there are numerous options available for providing coverage. Take the time to explore any and every alternative.

At the very least, you should have catastrophic coverage for those unforeseen events that could rob you of everything you own. Make sure your preferred health care provider and hospital are in the network of the plan you choose. People go bankrupt every day because they can't afford to pay their medical bills, and that's not right. Premiums are out of control, as are health care costs. Something has got to give, and I wish I had the answer.

LONG-TERM CARE INSURANCE

Once you've reached sixty-five years of age, there is about a 50 percent chance that you'll require long-term care someday. Long-term care insurance policies cover many of the nursing home, assisted living, and home care expenses not covered by Medicare. Other covered services typically include assistance with routine daily activities like eating, bathing, and dressing. The cost of these policies is not for the faint of heart, simply making them unaffordable for most Americans. If you can afford the premiums and get started early in life—say in your 40s or 50s—it is certainly worth considering. If, on the other hand, you follow the recipe outlined in this book, you should be able to fund these expenses from the net worth you have amassed.

PROPERTY AND CASUALTY INSURANCE

If you have a car, chances are your state requires you to have auto insurance. Reducing your premiums by going with higher deductibles makes sense if you are successfully funding an emergency savings fund. If a fender bender happens, you can use this money to satisfy your deductible. Be sure to stay with high-quality carriers, checking competitive rates annually to make sure that what you are paying is not out of line.

You are required to have property and casualty insurance on your home and its contents if you are a homeowner with a mortgage. Even if there is not a mortgage on your home, you should still have insurance.

RENTERS INSURANCE

Buy renters insurance if you're renting. Your landlord might require it anyway. It's affordable, covers losses to personal property, provides liability coverage if someone is injured while in your home, and covers your belongings when you travel. Do your homework on the discounts available, the amount of the deductible, and coverage limits.

UMBRELLA LIABILITY INSURANCE

Umbrella liability insurance is frequently an oversight, as it is rarely required. That said, it offers a lot of bang for the buck, providing extra coverage that goes over and above the liability limits of your home and auto policy, and it's relatively inexpensive. Many of the claim limits in place are not sufficient in specific circumstances, such as a loss of life. Make sure your umbrella liability policy includes your vehicle. A colleague of mine found out after many years that his umbrella liability policy didn't cover his car. He was livid, and when asked, the agent told him it was available but would have cost him an extra $20 a year. Some people.

◆

Have you taken the time to review your insurance needs?

Do you regularly compare prices?

Are you clear as to what insurance you own and why you have it?

Do your homework and exercise prudence concerning your insurance needs.

CHAPTER 29

GET EDUCATED ON EDUCATION

> *Education is what remains after you have forgotten everything you learned in school.*
>
> —Anonymous

With tuition continuing to escalate far faster than inflation and wages, the cost of college may be yet another expense staring you in the face. The total amount of outstanding student loans reached an all-time high of $1.41 trillion in 2019, eclipsing credit card debt. The amount of student loan debt is now second only to mortgage debt in the United States.

People have different philosophies on who should bear the cost of a college education. Some feel an obligation to fund their children's education, and others believe the financial responsibility belongs to the student. Regardless of who is footing the bill, there are strategies available that you and your children can implement to mitigate the expense of college.

If your children make good grades and stay out of trouble, they may qualify for grants and scholarships—virtually free money that they do not have to pay back. There are merit-based scholarships awarded for academic or athletic performance, and there are need-based scholarships based on the parents' ability to contribute. Regardless of your children's academics, their athletic prowess, and your financial standing, you and your children are going to have to roll up your sleeves and learn the rules of the game. Scholly (myscholly.com) is one platform that matches student profiles with available scholarship offers. It currently comes at a nominal cost of $2.99 a month. There is, frankly, a lot of money out there waiting for qualified students to grab, and digging for this treasure trove can be a worthwhile pursuit. If your children take Advanced Placement (AP) classes in high school, they can likely receive college credit for their efforts, thereby shortening the time they need to graduate. Another critical factor to consider is the difference between in-state and out-of-state tuition, which can vary dramatically.

If you intend to pay for your children's college education, there are several options to explore. Obviously, the sooner you start investing for college, the more realistic your chances are of achieving it. *Coverdell Education Savings Accounts* (also known as ESAs) offer flexible investment options, but the annual contribution is limited to only $2,000. As a result, they are no longer in fashion and may well be on their way out.

There is also the option of funding a traditional *custodial account*, but the drawbacks are many. The gift is irrevocable, and once the child reaches the age of majority (eighteen in most states), it belongs to them, even if your child abandons the idea of college altogether. Need-based financial aid is also adversely affected because the assets technically belong to the child.

A *529 plan* is a better investment vehicle for funding your child's college. There are two types of 529 plans: savings plans and prepaid tuition plans. I will focus on the savings plans, as they are by far the most popular. With a

529 plan, parents make after-tax contributions sponsored by the state, with the child as beneficiary. Some states allow a full or partial tax deduction. The contribution limits are high (up to $15,000 in 2020 per parent without being subject to gift tax), and the growth is tax-free as long as you withdraw the money for educational purposes. Furthermore, you can contribute a lump sum of up to $75,000 (five years' contribution) and treat this gift as being made over a five-year basis for gift-tax purposes.

With a 529 plan, you have the option to change the beneficiary. If your oldest child decides to ride off into the sunset on her boyfriend's Harley and forgo the college experience altogether, you retain the ability to change the beneficiary to any other member of the original beneficiary's family. Importantly, the money in 529 plans remains the property of the parent, making a significant difference when calculating financial aid. Also, know that you don't need to invest in the 529 plan offered by the state in which you reside. Any state's program will suffice, and you should choose one that includes the investment options and tax benefits that make the most sense.

But a 529 plan alone might not be your best or only option, and I have a stellar idea if you want to maintain control and flexibility. If you meet the income qualifications required to fund a Roth IRA, you should consider this option. As of 2020, if a single parent has a modified adjusted gross income (MAGI) not exceeding $124,000, or $196,000 for married couples filing jointly, they can contribute 100 percent of earned income up to $6,000 ($7,000 if fifty or older) per year. You can treat the withdrawals on a first-in, first-out (FIFO) basis. In other words, the first withdrawals are treated as a return on the principal and are not subject to income taxes.

For example, let's assume that you contributed $6,000 a year for fifteen years to a Roth IRA. The account value has grown to $225,000, of which you contributed $90,000, and the other $135,000 represents the gains. The $90,000 in contributions is readily available for tax-free withdrawal, and the $135,000 in profits will continue to grow tax-free. As with the 529 plan, the assets are the property of the parents, and they retain control. Any money not withdrawn for college expenses can go toward augmenting your retirement savings.

The sooner you begin to save, the more likely you will accomplish your goal. Time, once again, is your biggest ally. If you haven't saved enough money for your child's college education, there is always the student loan option. These are readily available as both subsidized and unsubsidized loans. Subsidized loans, available to those with financial need, do not accrue interest until six months after your child has graduated. Unsubsidized loans accrue interest while your child is in college, and that interest adds to the principal amount after graduation.

There are many tools available to lessen the blow of college tuition. Familiarize yourself with all of them and proceed in an orderly fashion.

◆

Do you feel responsible for funding for your children's college? If so, have you begun putting money away to fund it?

If you plan to invest for your children's college, start now.

CHAPTER 30

BUDGET
IS NOT A FOUR-LETTER WORD

>> *A budget tells us what we can't afford, but it doesn't keep us from buying it.*

—William Feather

I know many talented poker players who went bust because they didn't have a plan. They entered tournaments with a buy-in that was too large or played in cash games with stakes that were too high for their bankroll. Their confidence told them they could play with the big dogs when their net worth and poker-playing talent told a much different story.

Consummate poker professionals, on the other hand, have unique strategies for budgeting. They are careful not to overextend their resources, often mitigating and diversifying their exposure by selling a percentage of their winnings to outsiders.

CBS MarketWatch reported on August 19, 2016, that more than two-thirds of Americans don't have a budget. In 2015, the Bureau of Labor Statistics reported that nearly 38.5 percent of American households spend more than they earn. These numbers are undoubtedly related.

Let's be honest. If you're like most Americans, you are spending more than you're saving and slipping deeper and deeper into debt each month. You may have no money left at the end of the month to save or invest. Spending today without much thought about saving for tomorrow can become a pattern that will never allow you to get ahead financially. You can break this pattern, but it will take discipline, planning—and a budget.

Yes, you should have a budget. Without committing yourself to a budget, you have little chance of achieving financial success. This critical first step is needed to begin the practice of rigorous self-honesty regarding your money issues. Get the numbers down on paper, and you'll have a clear picture of your financial status. If you don't want to know where you stand, then don't create a budget. However, if you continue to live in some fantasy world wrapped in denial and avoid the issue entirely, financial progress is highly unlikely. Wishes and dreams won't do you a bit of good unless you take a hard look at your situation and then take the necessary steps to get where you want to go.

Having a budget will prompt you to differentiate your needs from your wants. Asking whether you want or need something before handing over your money to get it can save you from excessive spending. What is truly important to you: having that leather jacket in the store window or building a financially secure future? Do you *need* that leather jacket, or could you continue to wear the one you have? If you are willing to ignore some wants now, you will secure the financial resources you'll need in the future.

What is the best way to begin budgeting? Track your expenses for a month and figure out where your money is going. For the old-school crowd, dedicate a small notebook to this project, and record every dollar spent. For those of you more technologically inclined, Mint is a free budgeting application that works quite well. There are many other similar applications from which to choose. If you are new to this, expect to be both embarrassed and enlightened. You will be astounded by how much money you have been spending on fancy coffees without having a second thought. These expenses add up. There are countless ways to spend your hard-earned money that leave you with little or nothing to show for it. It's time to start paying attention to where your dollars have been going.

My oldest daughter came to me for financial advice shortly after graduating college. She was making terrific money, paying a modest rent, and didn't have a car payment, yet she routinely ended up with just a few dollars left in her bank account by the time the next payday rolled around. She could not understand for the life of her where her money was going. After a few months of tracking her expenses, she was excited to have her answer. She discovered that she was spending a whopping $1,500 a month on trivial things: a new blouse she didn't need, bottled water, and all-to-frequent restaurant visits. It's so easy to five-dollar yourself to death. Those Abraham Lincolns can add up. She started paying attention to how she was spending her money, adjusted her spending accordingly, and became a saver. She has made conscientious budgeting a habit, and it continues to serve her well.

Having and sticking to a budget doesn't mean you'll be cutting all the fun from your life and implementing extreme austerity measures. It means you will put your financial obligations and goals ahead of impulsive or mindless spending. Sticking to your budget may involve learning to cook instead of eating out or ordering prepared meals so habitually. You might surprise yourself at how good a cook you are. Reimagine eating out as a luxury, not a regular feature of your day. Likewise, you may find that you don't need a new car every three years and that getting a raise doesn't mean you need a bigger house.

Short-term decisions have long-term consequences that people often don't realize until it's too late. Think before you spend your money on those daily designer coffees, lottery tickets, tchotchkes, clothes, or countless toys for your kids—anything you don't need. There will always be somebody or something out there wanting to separate you from your money. Get smarter.

If you have never budgeted, the thought of doing so is probably uncomfortable and overwhelming, but over time what seems like a struggle will become an unconscious habit, as will living within your means. Fiscally responsible budgeting will enable you to grow your savings and expand your portfolio. People are often astonished at how easy it is to live within their means once they decide to do so. The extra money, compounded over your lifetime, will go a long way toward ensuring a comfortable retirement. With a well-planned and well-executed budget, you will unearth the funds you need for saving and investing.

Start tracking your spending, and consider your purchases more carefully, especially the sale items or fun things that seem too inexpensive to matter. It's your money, and it matters whether you throw it away or invest it for your future.

Until living within your means becomes routine, nothing I share in this book about effective money management will make any difference in your quest for financial success.

♦

Have you ever had a budget?

If not, does the thought of having one make you feel nauseous?

Are you willing to take on this new and essential habit?

Maintaining a sensible budget

is the foundation

of intelligent financial management.

CHAPTER 31

THE FUEL

" *There is no dignity quite so impressive, and no independence quite so important, as living within your means.*

—Calvin Coolidge

Professional poker players often caution that scared money never wins, and I agree. If you're going to gamble, make sure that you are doing so with money you can afford to lose. There have been more than a few instances when I have played poker against less-talented players who were risking their rent money at the table. It should go without saying that this is a poor way to manage money. I would not want to be their landlord.

Everyone seems to be looking for that panacea for all their financial woes. What company is going to be the next Apple Computer or Google or Amazon? I don't have a clue. What I do know is that spending less than you earn is the only surefire way to improve your finances. After you've paid your bills, you must have money left over to save and invest. I call this money FUEL.

If you're like most people, you have debt. Except for your mortgage, you should eliminate debt once and for all. Debt is the consequence of not living within your means, and there is no more significant roadblock you can face in accumulating wealth. I speak from my own experience and that of individuals I have advised. I have often joked that some people would rather confide in me about the extra-marital affair they were having than share with me how much they owe Visa. There is more truth in this statement than humor. Debt carries with it a lot of shame and denial. If you can change your mindset about debt, it will foster self-esteem, eradicate shame, and improve your experience immeasurably.

There are many theories about how to pay off debt, and I have mine as well. First, stop using credit cards and compounding your problem. If you must use them for transactions like renting a car, making a large purchase, or an unforeseen emergency, do your best to pay those charges off in full when you receive your bill. Create a budget for debt reduction that includes paying more than just your total minimum payments. You will need to reduce your spending elsewhere to make room for this budget item.

Pay off the debts with the highest interest first and start now. Use any windfalls you receive, including tax refunds, to further reduce your debt. Paying off high-interest debt is a better investment than anything I have up my sleeve. If you have a credit card with an interest rate of 15 percent, look at paying it off as being the equivalent of an investment with a guaranteed 15 percent after-tax return. You must get a handle on your relationship with debt, and when you do, your long-term plans will not only be achievable but a piece of cake.

Here's another simple piece of advice. If you can't afford it, don't buy it. This maxim alone will go a long way toward keeping you from creating unnecessary debt. Unfortunately, overspending continues to be the way people roll, and thus this advice bears repeating.

I am not suggesting that you become like Beans, driving the same car for thirty years and never taking a vacation. Nor do I want you to emulate Archie Karas and unconsciously commit to staying broke. There is a lot of room in between these two extremes.

I like the 50:30:20 budget rule. It's simple to follow. Fifty percent of your after-tax income is for essentials like housing and food, 30 percent is for discretionary spending, and 20 percent is for FUEL. Why 20 percent? With this percentage, using conservative assumptions of income increases and investment returns, it will take you approximately thirty years to create a *nest egg* equal to twenty-five times your income. If and when the time comes for you to stop working, you should be able to safely withdraw 4 percent of your nest egg every year with the added comfort of knowing that your money should last longer than you do, which is what most of us desire.

Perhaps this seems overly restrictive and that you could never afford to make this adjustment. Back a few years ago, the brother of a close friend of mine had just graduated from college and secured an entry-level job in the technology space with a starting salary of $40,000—a decent chunk of change at the time. He asked my advice on what percentage of his salary he should contribute to his 401(k), and I told him that 15 percent would be a smart move—an investment of $6,000 a year. Because it is a pre-tax investment, he would be reducing his after-tax income by approximately $4,500 a year, or only $375 a month. "I can't afford to do that," he moaned. I had to remind him that a month earlier, he was cutting my grass for spending money. I'm not sure what he ended up doing with his money other than buying a $2,000 king-size bed and a $1,500 TV. You get my point. Make saving a priority.

There is absolutely no reason why you cannot live on 80 percent of what you earn. Let me repeat that. There is absolutely no reason you cannot live on 80 percent of what you bring home. You may have to refrain from buying that new dress you saw in the window or forgo eating out every other night, but once you begin to treat that 20 percent like it's unavailable for spending, it will become easier.

This 20 percent represents the FUEL available for debt reduction, an emergency savings fund, and investments. I will get more detailed later in the book, but suffice it to say for now that saving 20 percent of your after-tax income is an excellent place to start. If that number seems implausible at this juncture, start saving something and gradually work your way up. You will find it easier than you thought.

More details to follow in the section on execution.

◆

Do your current spending habits come anywhere close to a 50:30:20 budget rule?

Can you adopt a growth mindset by saving a certain percentage of your income and making it a routine?

Make the necessary sacrifices

to live on no more

than 80 percent of your after-tax income.

CHAPTER 32

YOU SHOULD BE COMMITTED

> *Until one is committed, there is hesitancy, the chance to draw back, always ineffectiveness.*
>
> —William Hutchison Murray

Achieving financial freedom has more to do with commitment and execution than anything monetary. Many people talk a good game, but their plans never materialize because they lack the commitment and dedication required to implement those plans. Commitment fosters the perseverance you'll need to ensure your goals come to fruition. At some point in your life, you need to make a no-excuses-allowed commitment to becoming financially free. Now would be a good time.

While most of us desire financial freedom, only a small percentage of us take the steps necessary to achieve the desired result. Commitment is the secret sauce that bridges the gap between knowledge and implementation. The road to financial freedom requires that you be honest with yourself, recognize where you are, acquire the education you need, acknowledge your strengths and weaknesses, and remain steadfast in the pursuit of your financial goals. Don't make it complicated. Just do it. Start at the beginning and plow your way through.

A close friend of mine began running relatively late in life and before long became a champion marathoner. She set a goal of completing a marathon in each of the fifty states as well as all seven continents, and the last I heard, she is more than halfway there. Her commitment is resolute, and there is little doubt in my mind that she will get it done, no matter what it takes. She accepts no excuses from herself. I asked her one day to tell me her secret. She shared that her quest started a few years earlier when she decided to lace up her shoes and run around the block. Before long, she was running several miles. To me, running 26.2 miles is on par with climbing Mt. Everest, but she said running long distances wasn't all that difficult; it just took commitment

and laser focus. Once she could run five miles without stopping, working her way up to marathon distance was a piece
of cake.

Rome wasn't built in a day. It takes time, and regardless of where you are right now, it's a worthwhile pursuit
to work toward financial independence. "Well begun is half
done," says Aristotle. I agree wholeheartedly.

♦

*Do you have a habit of beginning projects and not seeing them
through?*

Is it easy for you to feel overwhelmed?

*Has the idea of financial success been little more than a pipe
dream?*

Make the unwavering commitment necessary to take what you have learned and put it into practice.

CHAPTER 33

THE MISSING LINK

> *I have been impressed with the urgency of doing. Knowledge is not enough; we must apply. Being willing is not enough; we must do.*
>
> —Leonardo da Vinci

You can read all the best books on how to play poker, but until you sit down at a table and play against real people for real money, you haven't even gotten started. The time you invest reading and acquiring poker knowledge will undoubtedly help, but it will not serve you well if you don't play the game. Don't allow that to happen with the knowledge you glean from this book. The ideas and concepts presented here are sound, and they will produce fruit. But will you execute them?

We know that eating healthy food and exercising produces both physical and mental benefits. We also know what happens if we consume mass quantities of junk food and if our exercise regimen is little more than rolling out of bed each morning. It's not rocket science. If you don't put your knowledge to work, you will fall short of achieving the desired result. The same is true when it comes to money matters. What's missing is a deeper understanding of the disconnect between knowing and doing. Bridging this chasm separates the winners from the losers. It's certainly not a lack of information.

In business, many companies fail to traverse the *knowing-doing gap* and, knowing that they need to make changes, hire one consultant after another, talk about ways to improve, but ultimately change nothing. Don't be like them.

I have this sign on the wall in my office: *Those who talk should do, and only those who do should talk.*

Talking is talking. Doing is doing.

Fear certainly plays a part, particularly the fear of what's around the corner. While we can maintain some degree of control in the short term, the future is anybody's guess. If we go out on a limb, we might fail. Then we'll feel guilty and shelve the idea altogether. A life of avoiding failure is boring and unproductive. My failures have taught me immeasurably more than my successes.

In my career of coaching individuals how to achieve a comfortable retirement, the cold, hard facts are often so overwhelming and seemingly unachievable that they don't even want to talk about it. Oh the number of times I've heard a client transition the conversation to an upcoming golf vacation in Pinehurst! Don't be like them. Sticking your head in the sand produces nothing but more anxiety and uncertainty.

Whatever your fears are, acting on them is the best medicine. If you have to start small by taking baby steps, then take baby steps. Just get started doing something. Like becoming a runner, the first few steps are the most difficult, but I promise it gets easier over time.

If you want to learn a foreign language, start studying.

If you've always wanted to learn to play guitar, buy one and take some lessons.

If you want to lose weight, eat fruits and vegetables instead of cake.

Knowledge is essential, but without the appropriate

action, it is worthless. If you genuinely desire to retire with the money you need to do what you please, simply follow the steps outlined in the following section on execution. Get busy.

◆

Do you have a history of being all talk and no action?

Does the future terrify you?

Are you willing to start now and act?

It's time to convert your knowledge into action.

CHAPTER 34

KNOWLEDGE RECAP

> " *Give me six hours to chop down a tree, and I will spend the first four sharpening the axe.*
>
> —Abraham Lincoln

As promised, I have separated the good, the bad, and the ugly. Know what to avoid, and cull your investment choices down to a smaller universe. Keep it simple. To summarize:

- ♣ Know the players in the game and recognize their designations for what they indeed are.
- ♣ Don't allow the daily news cycle to dictate your investment decisions.
- ♣ Quantify the rake and its effect on your bottom-line performance. Determine whether you are getting value for the fees you pay.
- ♣ If you're going to hire an investment adviser, ask a lot of questions.

♣ Limit your stock investments to passive ETFs.

♣ Limit your bond investments to passive ETFs.

♣ Determine the retirement plan(s) that you are eligible to participate in and familiarize yourself with the particulars.

♣ Take annuities off the table.

♣ Pass on the free steak dinner.

♣ Avoid bad bets and stick with the winners.

♣ Being a renter or the owner of a small home can be a smart move. Ignore groupthink, and scrutinize the pros and cons.

♣ Get your insurance life in order. Stuff happens.

♣ Plan for education expenses by starting early. Pursue every opportunity available to mitigate the cost.

♣ Budget.

♣ FUEL is mandatory to fund investments. Find it.

♣ Commit to the plan.

♣ Be the person who bridges the gap between knowledge and execution.

Simplify your life by confining your investment choices to cost-effective and proven winners.

EXECUTION

CHAPTER 35

FOLLOW THE RECIPE

" *Numbers don't lie. Women lie, men lie, but numbers don't.*

—Max Holloway

Las Vegas has fabulous restaurants featuring nearly every cuisine on the planet, and fine dining is a pleasure I include on every trip to the desert.

I enjoy the reputation in some circles of being a surprisingly good cook, but you won't find me cooking on TV anytime soon—or telling you the perfect spice mix for a dish, for that matter. Great chefs, on the other hand, have extensive knowledge of how to transform a run-of-the-mill dinner into a savory delight. They put their talents to work.

But for those without serious culinary skills, what's the secret to preparing a great meal? Recipes. (I know this book is supposed to be about personal finance, but stick with me here.) Proper guidance allows you to follow in the footsteps of chefs who, through trial and error, have demonstrated their ability to turn an ordinary dish into something extraordinary. I have learned the difference between a cup and a tablespoon. Sauté and braise are now a part of my lexicon. Between the internet and a few cookbooks, I have an endless list of recipes from which to choose. I search for something that sounds tasty and looks fun to make, buy whatever ingredients I don't have on hand, and then follow the directions. It's a piece of cake.

Don't be one of those people with all the information you need at your disposal and yet somehow fail to act. If you have been that person, change. What follows is a recipe for designing and managing your financial affairs. To get started, you can't just follow along. You have to do it! You may need to learn a few new words and adopt some better habits, but the payoff is enormous. You owe it to yourself and your loved ones to become a good steward of your money. There is no reason to be afraid—the cake is easy to make after the first or second try. I have intentionally made the recipe simple enough for anyone to follow.

◆

Are you coachable?

If so, preheat your oven, and let's begin making that perfect meal.

Being coachable,

even if it makes you feel vulnerable,

is the secret to achieving many

or most of your dreams.

CHAPTER 36

THE END GAME

> *What you get by achieving your goals is not as import-*
> *ant as what you become by achieving your goals.*
>
> —Zig Ziglar

Given you are (or at least should be) planning for retirement, let's peer into the finances of imaginary couple Harold and Maude Stevens and calculate how much net worth,
or nest egg, they will need to accumulate by retirement age.
This nest egg will provide them with the income they desire to remain comfortable for the remainder of their lives.

Harold and Maude are married, gainfully employed,
and thirty-five years of age. They have taken the time to
create a clear vision of what they want their retirement life
to look like but are struggling with how to make it happen.
Let's ask them some questions and imagine their answers.

"When would you like to retire?"

"In thirty years at age sixty-five," they say together.

"Great! If you were retiring tomorrow, how much money would you need to withdraw monthly from your nest egg to provide you with the lifestyle you desire?"

Harold and Maude look at each other for a moment, and then Maude chimes in with an estimate. "Four thousand dollars?"

With this information, planning becomes pretty straightforward. Multiply the Stevens' monthly income goal of $4,000 by twelve to get their annual income goal of $48,000. A conservative yearly *withdrawal rate* of 4 percent from the investor's nest egg should provide them with a high level of confidence that they will not outlive their money. An easy shortcut to calculate the funds required to provide this income is to multiply the annual income goal by twenty-five. Using this example, they would multiply $48,000 by twenty-five, which equals $1.2 million. Put another way, a 4 percent annual withdrawal rate on a $1.2 million nest egg will generate $48,000 a year in income. Keep in mind that this income is on top of social security benefits, pension benefits, and any inheritance they may be entitled to down the road.

But wait. There's more. Harold and Maude need to factor in the effects of inflation. A dollar isn't worth what it used to be, and it will be worth even less thirty years from now. Given the current economic environment, I assume and factor in an inflation rate of 3 percent for my calculations. Therefore, I would adjust the $1.2 million for inflation by compounding it at 3 percent annually over 30 years—that's just shy of $3 million.

Therefore, Harold and Maude Stevens will need to accumulate a nest egg of $3 million in thirty years —also referred to as their *Point B*—to begin withdrawing an inflation-adjusted income of $4,000 a month (see Table 1).

Review the calculations above as many times as necessary until they make sense to you. If math is not your forte, be patient, grab a calculator, and invest some time here. You can learn this.

Now, make the same calculations for your situation to determine your Point B (see Table 2).

Table 1 - Harold and Maude Stevens
Nest Egg Calculation

Number of years until retirement	30
Monthly income desired if they retire tomorrow ($)	4 000
Multiply by 12 to get	X 12
Annual income desired if they retire tomorrow ($)	48 000
Multiply by 25 to get	X 25
Nest egg required if they retire tomorrow ($)	1 200 000
Adjust the nest egg required tomorrow by an inflation rate of 3% to get the nest egg they will require in 30 years ($)	2 912 715

Table 2 - Your
Nest Egg Calculation

Number of years until retirement	12
Monthly income desired if you retire tomorrow ($)	12,800
Multiply by 12 to get	X 12
Annual income desired if you retire tomorrow ($)	153,600
Multiply by 25 to get	X 25
Nest egg required if you retire tomorrow ($)	3,840,000
Adjust the nest egg required tomorrow by an inflation rate of 3% to get the nest egg you will require in 12 years ($)	5,599,990. 5.6 millions

To get your inflation-adjusted income, use the compound interest calculator on my favorite number-crunching website, www.thecalculatorsite.com. Visit this site, learn it, and bookmark it for later use.

While building a nest egg sufficient to provide the income you desire at retirement may seem out of reach, let me assure you that this is an achievable goal if you follow the recipe outlined in the following pages.

◆

Can you follow a recipe?

Does this math make sense to you?

Calculate your Point B.

CHAPTER 37

THE STARTING BLOCKS

" *The best time to plant a tree was twenty years ago. The second-best time is now.*

—Chinese Proverb

Now that you have determined your Point B, the next step is to calculate your current *net worth*—the value of your assets minus your liabilities. I refer to this as your *Point A.* That means it's time to crunch a few more numbers.

Let's begin by analyzing Harold and Maude Stevens' current net worth by first adding up their assets and liabilities. When they subtract their total liabilities from their total assets, the difference represents their net worth. Their current financial statement shows assets of $459,000 and liabilities of $259,000. After subtracting liabilities from assets, their resultant net worth is $200,000 (see Table 3).

Table 3 - Harold and Maude Stevens

Net Worth Statement

Assets	$	Liabilities	$
Home	350 000	Mortgage	250 000
Autos	20 000	Auto loans	6 000
Emergency savings	9 000	Credit cards	3 000
Investments	50 000		
Personal belongings	30 000		
Total	459 000		259 000
Net worth (assets minus liabilities)	200 000		

Let's further assume that Harold and Maude have a joint gross income of $120,000 and an after-tax (net) income of $90,000. They have their starting point of $200,000, their ending point of $3 million, and their time frame of thirty years.

You may have done a similar calculation at your bank or when applying for a mortgage. That's Harold and Maude's Point A calculation, but now let's do the same for you (see Table 4).

Table 4 - Your
Net Worth Statement

Assets	$	Liabilities	$
Home	450,000.	Mort.	200,000.
CAsh	127,000.		
Autos	25,000.		
Stock	640,000.		
Personal	30,000.		
Total	1.272 mil		200,000,
Net worth (assets minus liabilities)	1,072,000. 1.072 mil		

On the left side, itemize all of your assets, including the market value of your home and automobiles, your investments, your bank deposits, and the resale value of any personal property you could easily convert to cash. Total the value of your assets.

On the right side, itemize all of your liabilities, including your mortgage, auto loans, and credit card debt. Total the value of your liabilities.

Your net worth—your Point A—is equal to your assets minus your liabilities.

The next piece of information necessary to create your financial plan is to calculate your income. If you are married, combine the numbers to get your *joint income.*

You have now determined your Point A, Point B, time frame, and your current income. In the next chapter, we'll start connecting the dots.

◆

Have you completed a simple statement of your current net worth?

Are you excited to see how you can get from Point A to Point B?

Know how to calculate your net worth at any given point in time.

CHAPTER 38

THE 50:30:20 BUDGET RULE

What gets measured gets managed.

—Peter Drucker, recipient of the Presidential Medal of

Freedom

It's time to review Harold and Maude Stevens' finances. To remind you, here is the broad overview:

- ♣ Their Point A is $200,000.
- ♣ Their Point B is $3,000,000.
- ♣ Their time frame is 30 years.
- ♣ Their current after-tax joint income is $90,000.

Do you remember the 50:30:20 budget rule from earlier? Let's break it down for them (see Table 5).

Now let's do the same for you. It's time to put your budget to work. While essential and discretionary expenses will vary, together, they should not exceed 80 percent of your after-tax income. Look over last year's payments (or at least payments from the past three months) and see how well you conformed to the 50:30:20 budget rule. If your current budget allows for a FUEL allocation of 20 percent or higher, congratulations! If not, you will need to make the necessary adjustments to your spending habits to procure the FUEL you need (see Table 6).

Successful businesses function this way. Every household should be looked at much like a small business—revenue coming through the door, expenses going out, and (hopefully) some level of profit left over at the end of the day. Budgeting does not have to be complicated, but it can be if that's your thing. When I began doing this practice many years ago, I started off using way too many categories and subcategories, and the whole ordeal became taxing and required way too much thinking. It was, however, quite illuminating and taught me where my money was going and how I was frittering it away. Now, if breaking down each of the three main categories into smaller and smaller subsets is how you roll, so be it.

Table 5 - *Harold and Maude Stevens*
50:30:20

	Yearly ($)	Monthly ($)
Gross income	120 000	10 000
Net income	90 000	7 500
Essentials like housing and food (50%)	45 000	3 750
Discretionary spending (30%)	27 000	2 250
Fuel (20%)	18 000	1 500

Table 6 - *Your*
50:30:20

	Yearly ($)	Monthly ($)
Gross income	215,000.	17,900.
Net income *Less taxes And Health Ins.*	144,000;	12,000.
Essentials like housing and food (50%) *Mort, Food*	72,000.	6,000,
Discretionary spending (30%)	43,200,	3,600.
Fuel (20%)	28,800.	2,400.

Today I prefer to keep my budgeting relatively pain-less by making a simple distinction between whether an expenditure is essential or discretionary. At the end of the month, I total my income, subtract my necessary and discretionary expenses, and apply the remainder to FUEL.

Although you may have never done anything like this before, it is a straightforward exercise that will be profound in the results it generates.

Important note: I am not recommending that you become obsessed with budgeting. The intent here is not to create a *scarcity mindset*, a belief that there will never be enough. Ironically, that kind of thinking can be counterproductive. It is crucial, however, to know where your money is going so that you can begin to look at other means to increase the money you have available for FUEL, be it by increasing revenue or decreasing expenses. Maybe there's an inheritance coming down the road.

Next, we will discuss what to do with your FUEL.

◆

Are your essential and discretionary expenses in line?

Are you consistently saving?

Have you been running low on FUEL?

Make the 50:30:20 budget rule a habit and find your FUEL.

RATIONING YOUR FUEL

““ *Life is not a matter of holding good cards, but some-times, playing a poor hand well.*

—Jack London

If you are following along and doing these calculations, you have now found your FUEL. Depending on your current financial situation, you will want to allocate this FUEL among three buckets—debt reduction, an emergency savings fund, and investments. Using Harold and Maude Stevens again as our test case, let's assume their net worth of $200,000 includes debt of $9,000, an emergency savings fund of $9,000, and investments of $50,000 (see Table 7).

Based on their 50:30:20 budget rule calculations, Harold and Maude have committed and initially budgeted $18,000 for FUEL annually, or $1,500 a month. But how should this best be allocated?

Table 7 - Harold and Maude Stevens

Bucket Strategy

	Debt ($)	Emergency savings ($)	Invest- ments ($)
Point A ($)	9 000	9 000	50 000
Year 1 allocation (%)	50	25	25
Year 1 allocation ($)	9 000	4 500	4 500
Year 1 balance ($)	0	13 500	54 500
Year 2 allocation (%)	NA	50	50
Year 2 allocation ($)	NA	9 000	9 000
Year 2 balance ($)	0	22 500	63 500
Year 3 allocation (%)	NA	NA	100
Year 3 allocation ($)	NA	NA	18 000
Year 3 balance ($)	0	22 500	81 500

The first bucket is for debt reduction. If there is any debt outstanding, I recommend an initial allocation of 50 percent of the FUEL toward this first bucket to begin eliminating unsecured debt (not backed by an asset such as a home or automobile) and auto loans. In the case of Harold and Maude, this represents an allocation of $750 a month. They should pay the minimum amount on the auto loan (with the lower interest rate) and prioritize paying the credit card off. Always pay any extra dollars available to the debt with the highest interest rate.

Some of you have debt, and some of you do not. Some of you have been to hell and back with it. While it can take no time to amass a mountain of debt, it can take decades to pay it back. Immediate gratification is your archenemy, and if you continue to succumb to its myriad temptations, you will significantly stifle your ability to create significant wealth over the long term. If you have unsecured debts such as credit cards, you need to get rid of them. Period. End of story. No excuses. No matter how long it takes. Going forward, you must exercise discipline and stringently evaluate the potential repercussions of further borrowing.

Good credit history can go a long way toward lowering your interest rate if you need to borrow money. You can often save on your auto and home insurance premiums if your credit score is high. In general, you should reserve the use of debt for leveraging appreciating assets (such as a mortgage on a home), not for purchasing depreciating assets like a new car or a vacation. Poor credit history, on the other hand, can affect your ability to get a job or even rent a desirable apartment.

Begin the process of evaluating and managing your credit history by going to www.annualcreditreport.com. This site will provide you with credit reports from Equifax, Experian, and TransUnion once a year at no cost. Review the statements carefully and dispute any incorrect items. Mistakes are commonplace. Clean them up.

The second bucket is for an emergency savings fund, which should contain a minimum of three months of after-tax income. This amount should be adequate in the event of unforeseen financial hardship. Keep this money in a liquid money market, or savings account at a financial institution. In the case of Harold and Maude, their emergency savings fund should contain a minimum of $22,500.

The third bucket is reserved for investments, prioritizing allocations to any company retirement plan, such as a 401(k) offering a match—where an employer makes contributions to the retirement plan equal to the employee's contributions. An immediate doubling of money is not a benefit to ignore.

An emergency savings fund should be funded with 25 percent of the FUEL until it accumulates to three months of after-tax income. Therefore, Harold and Maude should allocate 25 percent of their monthly FUEL, or $375 a month, until this account has reached its goal of $22,500.

The remaining balance of 25 percent should go toward investments.

Once the debt is retired, distribute the FUEL equally between the emergency savings fund and investments. When three months of after-tax income is sitting in an emergency savings fund, 100 percent of the FUEL then goes toward investments.

At the end of Year 1, Harold and Maude have completely retired their debt. Their emergency savings fund has grown from $9,000 to $13,500. Their investments have grown from $50,000 to $54,500, assuming there is no interest or change in investment values. With the debt completely retired, their FUEL is split equally between the remaining two buckets until they reach their emergency savings fund goal.

At the end of Year 2, the emergency savings fund reached its target of $22,500. Now that they have realized both the debt repayment and emergency savings fund goals,

100 percent of their FUEL can go to investments. They are well on their way!

Following the Stevens' example, plug in your numbers and craft your plan (see Table 8).

Table 8 – Your

Bucket Strategy

	Debt ($)	Emergency savings ($)	Investments ($)
Point A($)			
Year 1 allocation (%)			
Year 1 allocation ($)			
Year 1 balance ($)			
Year 2 allocation (%)			
Year 2 allocation ($)			
Year 2 balance ($)			
Year 3 allocation (%)			
Year 3 allocation ($)			
Year 3 balance ($)			

Envision how good it will feel having no unsecured debt, three months of after-tax income parked in an emergency savings fund, and all of your FUEL going into investments. Exciting, isn't it?

Do you understand the concept of rationing your FUEL?

Are you willing to forgo using debt to finance depreciating assets or vacations?

Are you beginning to see the light at the end of the tunnel?

Create the system for allocating your FUEL until 100 percent of it can go toward investments.

CHAPTER 40

GETTING FROM POINT A TO POINT B

" *Our goals can only be reached through the vehicle of a plan, in which we must fervently believe, and upon which we must vigorously act.*

—Pablo Picasso

A financial plan organizes how you handle money to take you from where you are (Point A) to where you want to go (Point B). It's that simple. This plan must be in writing and include specific dates and dollar amounts, with the understanding that it will probably need to be amended from time to time, as life has a habit of throwing us curveballs.

Again, in the case of Harold and Maude Stevens, we have the following data points:

- ♣ Their Point A is $200,000.
- ♣ Their Point B is $3,000,000.

♣ Their time frame is 30 years.

♣ Their current after-tax joint income is $90,000.

♣ Their initial annual FUEL of 20 percent is $18,000.

Is it even conceivable for them to achieve their Point B? Yes, it is, and I'm going to show you how. Let's crunch a few numbers.

Because we are factoring in an inflation rate of 3 percent, it should follow that our annual FUEL contribution should increase by 3 percent as well. Another assumption in this projection is that the investments will grow by 6 percent a year. We all know what *assume* means, but 6 percent is a pretty conservative number.

Using the compound interest calculator referenced earlier (www.thecalculatorsite.com), I made the following determination. If Harold and Maude Stevens contribute $18,000 to FUEL a year, increase that amount by 3 percent annually, and grow their investments at an average annual rate of 6 percent, they will end up with a net worth of $3.2 million in Year 30—exceeding their retirement goal (Point B) of $3 million!

Complete the same calculations for yourself using the same website.

♣ Enter your Point A in the Initial Balance box.

♣ Enter 6 percent in the Interest Rate box.

♣ Enter your time frame in the Calculation Period box.

♣ Enter Yearly in the Compound Interval box.

♣ Enter your monthly FUEL in the Regular Monthly Deposit/Withdrawal box.

♣ Check Increase Deposits Yearly with Inflation box, and enter 3 percent.

♣ Calculate.

If your time frame is shorter, you will need to contribute more to FUEL or expect a smaller Point B. A dose of reality won't kill you. Keep it real. If you get a raise, there is no commandment requiring you to raise your expenses proportionately. Bump up your FUEL allocation. Should you get a big windfall such as an inheritance or a smaller one like a tax refund, feed the lion's share of that money to FUEL, and shorten your time horizon.

Similar calculations can be made for other financial goals as well, such as saving for your children's college expenses, a second home, or maybe that trip around the world you've always wanted to make. As they say, you can't take it with you, so don't beat yourself up if you opt for a little immediate gratification now and then. Just don't let it become your spending ritual. There are rewards to come later from good financial habits practiced early. You might even start to enjoy it.

Keep reading to find out how to invest your money wisely so that your goals can become a reality.

◆

Have you learned how to use the compound interest calculator?

What revelations, if any, have you had?

Is your financial plan starting to come together?

Visualize and quantify your road from Point A to Point B.

CHAPTER 41

PLAYING THE GAME

> *Seek, above all, for a game worth playing. Such is the advice of the oracle to modern man. Having found the game, play it with intensity—play as if your life and sanity depend on it. They do depend on it. Follow the example of the French existentialists and flourish a banner bearing the word engagement. Though nothing means anything and all roads are marked No Exit, yet move as if your movements had some purpose. If life does not seem to offer a game worth playing, then invent one. For it must be clear, even to the most clouded intelligence, that any game is better than no game.*
>
> —Robert S. de Ropp, from *The Master Game*

Let me begin by saying that there is no perfect investment strategy, and people who claim to have such an approach are either disingenuous or drinking their own Kool-Aid.

The inspiration for writing this book came from observing how the behavior of poker players mirrored my experience with investment clients throughout my career. After a couple of hours at the tables, I had a pretty good idea about how the players handled their investments. The revelation just jumped right out at me.

One thing I've found, both in poker and in investing, is that winning over the long term requires patience devoid of emotion. It's indeed a grind, and the quicker you try to get to the finish line, the more unlikely you are to reach it. There is no perfect investment strategy. However, there are optimal ways to play the game. You're learning one by reading this book.

Poker is a game of people played with cards. When playing poker, especially in Las Vegas at a table of strangers, I make every attempt to find out where the other players live. Many are on vacation, and if so, I want to know. There are almost always a few locals (often retired) sitting at the table as well. Generally speaking, the difference in their styles of play is stark. Every time, chips slowly and methodically move from the vacationers to the locals. Remember our discussion on the cost of entertainment? Vacationers often unconsciously set themselves up for failure by playing until they are out of chips. They came to play, not to win.

Those on the other side of the table, though, aren't there for entertainment. They understand that prudent, methodical poker play is a grind. Though locals rarely win or lose any significant amount of money, their average daily take-home pay provides a sweet income stream that more than likely doesn't show up on their tax returns.

Shortly after selling my firm, I headed to Las Vegas and put a plan in motion, doing my best to emulate what I had gleaned from observing successful poker grinders. It worked. I played for ten grueling hours nearly every day. After three months of banking pretty decent and relatively predictable income while never exposing myself to any significant degree of risk, I decided that the money wasn't enough to justify sitting at a poker table for sixty hours a week. (Perhaps no amount of money is.) This experience taught me a lot about myself, and it became clear to me that this lifestyle was not going to be my future. I needed to spend some time outdoors and among friends and family. So I came home.

This adventure had profound effects on how I viewed the investment world. Besides being a recovered alcoholic, I am also a recovered *market timer*—one who continually moves money around trying to buy low and sell high. It was exhilarating, and I loved it. Sometimes it worked like a charm, and I looked like a genius. Other times I had a lot of egg on my face. Regardless, there was no shortage of adrenaline flowing through my veins. In contrast, the buy-and-hold strategy had always seemed to be a lazy and unsophisticated person's idea of how to make money in the stock market.

I eventually put my ego and the emotional roller coaster aside and joined the ranks of those who had concluded that there is no crystal ball and that markets are mostly efficient. While the short-term traders swinging for the fences thrive on the excitement and thrill of the hunt, the methodical, unemotional plodders eventually finish first. You should follow in their footsteps.

Nowadays, when short-term volatility (noise) occurs, I do my best to remain stoic. Thank you, Las Vegas, for teaching me this lesson. Boring can be a beautiful thing.

Now it's time to put some money to work.

◆

If you have a crystal ball, please list it for sale on eBay. People will buy anything.

Are you willing to ignore Uncle Louie's hot tips once and for all?

Will you check your ego at the door?

It's time in the market, not timing the market.

CHAPTER 42

WHERE TO INVEST

> *Don't gamble; take all your savings and buy some good stock and hold it till it goes up, then sell it. If it don't go up, don't buy it.*
>
> —Will Rogers

When investing your FUEL, begin with funding the retirement accounts that apply to your current situation. Remember that you can invest in these accounts on a pre-tax or after-tax basis. *Pre-tax accounts* are taxable when withdrawn in retirement, and *after-tax accounts* have no income taxes levied down the road. It's all but impossible to determine which is the best route, as many assumptions have to be made, like future income tax brackets, tax law changes, and earnings. I encourage you, if possible, to have money in both—a clever way of hedging your bets. You will have the option during retirement to withdraw from the one that is the most tax advantageous at the time.

Putting money to work in this way accomplishes several important things:

♣ If your contributions are pre-tax, that effectively lowers your taxable income and, in turn, your tax bill. You can increase the size of your contributions without impinging your immediate cash flow. For example, a $1,000 pre-tax investment will reduce the size of your paycheck by only $700, assuming a 30 percent marginal tax bracket.

♣ You benefit from *tax-deferred* earnings. With no current taxes siphoned off along the way, your money will accumulate faster. These investment vehicles include 401(k) plans, 403(b) plans, traditional IRAs, and Roth IRAs, among others.

♣ Company retirement plans typically operate on autopilot when it comes to funding. With contributions withdrawn automatically from each paycheck, the procedure becomes relatively painless and palatable. It's telling to see how quickly your current expenditures adjust to a decrease in the size of your paycheck. Additionally, having to decide whether or not to invest any given month can invite the imme-diate-gratification monster in your house to wreak havoc on your long-term plans.

♣ Withdrawals from qualified accounts before age fifty-nine and a half are added to your pre-tax in-come for that year and are subject to an additional 10 percent penalty. Most investors consider this to be a negative. Nonetheless, I would posit that the consequences of early withdrawals go a long way to-ward keeping you from foolishly pulling out money prematurely. Call it forced discipline.

♣ You can periodically rebalance your accounts to re-flect the proper allocation percentages (discussed later) without transaction costs or tax consequences. I prefer quarterly or annual rebalancing.

Qualifications and limits on retirement plans are ever changing and may well be obsolete by the time you read this. If you have a 401(k) or 403(b) plan offering a match, make sure to allocate FUEL to these first to take full advan-tage of the free money. After that, if you qualify, fund oth-er retirement plans depending on your income levels and whether or not you are self-employed. Retirement plans for self-employed individuals, such as SEP-IRAs, may offer significantly higher contribution limits than a traditional or Roth IRA.

When you have maxed out your retirement plan contributions, you can begin to invest in *nonqualified accounts*—accounts that do not qualify for any level of tax-deferred or tax-exempt status. An example would be an individual or joint investment account.

If you leave a company where you have a 401(k) or 403(b) plan, you will typically have three options:

1. Take a direct distribution of the entire account value. Pay the income tax, pay the 10 percent penalty if you're not yet a senior citizen, take a vacation, buy a bunch of stuff you don't need, and start your building your wealth all over again.

2. Keep your retirement account in the current plan, remain limited by the investment options available, and continue to pay comparatively high fees.

3. Execute a tax-deferred rollover into a self-directed IRA, open up your investment options, and invest in cost-effective ETFs.

If the answer is not yet abundantly clear, please read the options mentioned above again.

Your investments should be well diversified, and buying individual stocks is likely not in your best interest, no matter what Uncle Louie tells you. Your portfolio should be allocated, in a broader sense, to reflect your time frame. The longer your time frame is, the more volatility and risk you should be willing to accept. When you are contributing on a systematic basis, you also benefit from *dollar-cost averaging*. This strategy automatically buys more shares when the price is lower and fewer shares when the price is higher—effectively lowering your average cost per share without letting your emotions affect your play.

◆

Are you taking full advantage of any matching benefits you are entitled to?

How much money are you entitled to invest on a pre-tax basis?

Your primary allocation of investment FUEL should go to pre-tax accounts.

CHAPTER 43

HOW TO INVEST

> *People do not wish to appear foolish; to avoid the appearance of foolishness, they are willing to remain actually fools.*

—Alice Walker

In the world of investing, there is perhaps no concept as misunderstood as risk. It is a multifaceted issue, and your perception of and reaction to it can significantly influence your approach to investing.

Numerous questionnaires are available to help you determine your *risk profile*—the degree of variability in investment returns you are willing to withstand. If you have a high net worth and lots of disposable income, you may be willing to accept more risk than those of less substantial means.

As you know by now, I'm not a big fan of factoring in feelings when making investment decisions. Ergo, if you have a time horizon of twenty years and an aggressive portfolio doesn't provide the comfort level you desire, you might want to reconsider your thinking. In the majority of situations, your risk profile should reflect your *time horizon*—when you're expecting to need the money back. The younger you are, the more aggressive you can afford to be in your investment strategy. As you approach and eventually enter retirement, you will typically want to transition to a more conservative approach with your portfolio. The longer the time horizon, the more volatility you should be able to withstand.

I recommend the use of three different investment portfolios—with industry-standard names—depending on your time horizon:

- ♣ Far Better Aggressive (for time frames of more than ten years)

- ♣ Far Better Moderate (for time frames between five and ten years)

- ♣ Far Better Conservative (for time frames between two and five years)

If your time frame is less than two years, invest the money in a money market fund or savings account with no risk.

Aggressive portfolios are comprised mainly of stocks. In my recommended portfolio, it's 100 percent stocks. As time moves on and your time horizon shortens, bonds are added to mitigate volatility and risk, culminating in a conservative mix of 60 percent stocks and 40 percent bonds.

You need to pay attention to fees, as they can have a profoundly deleterious effect on the performance of your investment accounts. I prefer ETFs since they are well diversified and easy to buy and sell, plus their fees are so minuscule that they are of little consequence. The expense fees for my portfolios range from 0.06 to 0.07 percent. For example, a Far Better Moderate portfolio with an expense ratio of 0.07 percent will cost you only $70 annually for a $100,000 account. Many brokerage firms offer free trades these days, so $70 is your total cost!

The portfolios on the following pages are constructed with ETFs that are well diversified, trade a large volume of shares, and have low expense fees. The ETFs suggested can be bought in any self-directed IRA or traditional brokerage account. Allocating your investments in a 401(k) may be limited, however, so use the suggested ETF allocations as a guide. For example, you could substitute any large-cap value option offered in your 401(k) for the Vanguard Value ETF recommended. If there is not a choice that matches up well (perhaps there is no emerging-markets option), just allocate as best you can to emulate the ETFs suggested.

Begin the initial investing process by purchasing ten equally weighted positions—each representing 10 percent of the total account value. As you add more dollars, add to the position(s) with the lowest total value to keep the account percentages reasonably well balanced. There is no need to sell any of your holdings until reaching the time horizon needing the income. It's that simple.

◆

Are your investments well diversified?

Do your investment allocations reflect your time frame?

How much are you paying in expense fees?

Are you ready to drastically reduce the fees you're paying?

Establish a portfolio of ETFs reflecting your investment risk profile and time horizon.

CHAPTER 44

THREE PORTFOLIOS

I think that the first thing is that you should have a strategic asset allocation mix that assumes that you don't know what the future is going to hold.

—Ray Dalio

When determining your investing portfolio, the first step is to determine the allocation among US equities, international, equities, and fixed income (bonds) based on your time horizon (see Table 9).

Table 9 - Far Better Portfolio

Master

	Aggressive allocation (%)	Moderate allocation (%)	Conservative allocation (%)
US Equity	60	50	40
Non-US Equity	40	30	20
Fixed Income	0	20	40
Total	**100**	**100**	**100**

After that, the appropriate ETFs are chosen to complete the portfolio (see Tables 10, 11, and 12). Although there are different ETF providers recommended, you will find all of them available for purchase with any custodian, such as Fidelity or Schwab.

Diversified, low-cost, and tax-advantaged portfolios are the most prudent way to invest.

Table 10 - Far Better Portfolio - Aggressive

	ETF	Ticker
US Equity		
Large-Cap Blend	Schwab US Large-Cap	SCHX
Large-Cap Value	Vanguard Value	VTV
Small-Cap Blend	Schwab US Small-Cap	SCHA
Mid-Cap Blend	Schwab US Mid-Cap	SCHM
Small-Cap Value	Vanguard Small-Cap Value	VBR
Real Estate	Schwab US REIT	SCHH
Non-US Equity		
Foreign Large-Cap Blend	Schwab International Equity	SCHF
Emerging Markets	Schwab Emerging Markets Equity	SCHE
Foreign Small-Cap Blend	Schwab International Small-Cap Equity	SCHC
Foreign Large-Cap Value	iShares Core MSCI Total International Stock	IXUS

Table 11 - Far Better Portfolio
Moderate

	ETF	Ticker
US Equity		
Large-Cap Blend	Schwab US Large-Cap	SCHX
Large-Cap Value	Vanguard Value	VTV
Small-Cap Blend	Schwab US Small-Cap	SCHA
Mid-Cap Blend	Schwab US Mid-Cap	SCHM
Small-Cap Value	Vanguard Small-Cap Value	VBR
Non-US Equity		
Foreign Large-Cap Blend	Schwab International Equity	SCHF
Emerging Markets	Schwab Emerging Markets Equity	SCHE
Foreign Small-Cap Blend	Schwab International Small-Cap Equity	SCHC
Fixed Income		
Intermediate-Term Government Bond	Schwab Intermediate-Term US Treasury	SCHR
Long-Term Government Bond	Vanguard Long-Term Treasury	VGLT

Table 12 - Far Better Portfolio

Conservative

	ETF	Ticker
US Equity		
Large-Cap Blend	Schwab US Large-Cap	SCHX
Large-Cap Value	Vanguard Value	VTV
Small-Cap Blend	Schwab US Small-Cap	SCHA
Mid-Cap Blend	Schwab US Mid-Cap	SCHM
Non-US Equity		
Foreign Large-Cap Blend	Schwab International Equity	SCHF
Emerging Markets	Schwab Emerging Markets Equity	SCHE
Fixed Income		
Intermediate-Term Government Bond	Schwab Intermediate-Term US Treasury	SCHR
Long-Term Government Bond	Vanguard Long-Term Treasury	VGLT
Intermediate-Term Corporate Bond	Vanguard Intermediate-Term Corporate Bond	VCIT
High-Yield Bond	SPDR Bloomberg Barclays High Yield Bond	JNK

CHAPTER 45

YOU CAN BE A DIY INVESTOR

> *The role of the musician is to go from concept to full ex-*
> *ecution. Put another way, it's to go from understanding*
> *the content of something to really learn to communicate*
> *it and make sure it's well-received and lives in some-*
> *body else.*
>
> —Yo-Yo Ma

I attended a poker game one evening run by a married couple out of their home. I am in no way suggesting this as a
course of action, but in case you're curious, it can be quite
profitable to host a game like this, although not strictly legal. The revenue comes from the rake, and theirs was expensive. They were dragging 10 percent of every pot into
their coffers, capping the rake at $10 a hand. With a good
dealer, a table like this can deal about twenty-five hands an
hour. With an average rake of $8 a hand, we're talking $200

an hour per table per hour, and these games can go on until the sun rises. At ten hours of play, the house is taking in $2,000 for the session—and that's for a single table! With a headwind like that, every player could go home a loser. I didn't go back. They were friendly people, and the food was OK, but the cost of doing business was just too high.

If you take the time to study this book, reread it as often as necessary, and follow the recipes, you can create a fabulous meal without having to pay for the services of a Michelin-star chef. Many of you, on the other hand, will never consider managing your own money, and there's nothing wrong with that. Some people need help—or believe they do—and are willing to pay for it. I'm not here to judge.

Nonetheless, this book lays out everything you need to know to become a DIY investor. For those of you who are willing to learn, I've provided the direction. Perhaps this book was a gift from a frustrated spouse. Regardless, the following illustration might nudge a few of you to step outside of your comfort zone.

In calculating the growth in Harold and Maude Stevens' investment portfolio, assuming an annual growth rate of 6 percent, their projected Point B is over $3.2 million. Let's further assume that their 6 percent annual return was net of a 1 percent management fee paid to an adviser. Had they become DIY investors and instead received the full 7 percent annual return, would their Point B amount have changed significantly? At first glance, you might not think that just 1 percent would make that much difference. Let's compare, and you tell me. Increasing the net performance from 6 to 7 percent (using my favorite web-based calculator again), Harold and Maude's Point B skyrockets to $3,943,245, for a whopping increase of $740,725—nearly three-quarters of a million dollars! Maybe that will light a fire under your ass. Maybe not. I just thought you would want to know.

There are times, however, when it's necessary and advisable to pay a fee for more sophisticated services. Determining the optimum placement of your retirement dollars in an ever-changing tax landscape, for example, may require a level of expertise that the average investor doesn't have. However, paying a fee for services that you can so easily accomplish on your own is a cost you don't need to incur.

Robo-advisers—software programs for managing investment portfolios with low fees, low minimums, and a systematic approach to investing—are a relative newcomer to the investment arena. The first robo-adviser, Betterment, launched in 2010, and the concept has flooded the investment landscape, with subsequent offerings coming from big players like Vanguard and Charles Schwab.

By offering low fees and negligible minimums, robo-advisers take the emotion out of the investing process, which is always a good thing. In the Stevens example, had they used a robo-adviser with a fee of ½ percent, they would have achieved a net annual growth rate of 6.5 percent, which translates into a Point B of $3.5 million—an additional $300 thousand for that rainy day in retirement.

Of course, the downside here is that no human is involved apart from you. Many people contend that having the right adviser in the mix is both necessary and worth every dollar spent on fees and commissions. Robo-advisers can provide a happy medium or a steppingstone on the way to becoming a full-fledged DIY investor.

Be conscious of the fees you are paying, and make sure that you're getting a good bang for your buck. Be direct and don't shy away from asking questions.

If you still find yourself a little gun-shy, start by managing a small piece of your portfolio, work your way up, and build your confidence. Every person I know who has ventured down this path discovered that managing their investments was not all that difficult. Go ahead and stick your toe in the water. Even if it's a little cold, you'll get used to it, and the pay is excellent.

◆

Have you tried managing your money on your own?

Does the thought of doing so intimidate you?

Are you willing to take a stab at doing it yourself?

Step out of your comfort zone and become a DIY investor.

CHAPTER 46

COVER YOUR ASS

> *We have two lives, and the second one begins we realize we only have one.*
>
> —Confucius

Have you ever met a life insurance agent who didn't think you needed more life insurance? Asking a life insurance agent how much life insurance you need is like asking a barber if you need a haircut.

Life insurance certainly has its place and can be an intelligent and strategic component of your wealth-creation and wealth-preservation process. Finding a sweet spot between throwing your money away on unnecessary, expensive coverage and leaving your loved ones in jeopardy can be a confusing and daunting task. There are many schools of thought on the amount of life insurance you need, and I am not without my opinion.

Your estate primarily consists of your *life estate* (assets) and your *death estate* (life insurance). It represents the amount of money your beneficiaries will inherit in the event of your demise. In the early years of your life, the lion's share of your estate is your death estate, as building your life estate is just getting underway. Over time, your life estate becomes a more substantial portion of the whole, gradually replacing your death estate until becoming your entire estate.

What is the purpose of life insurance anyway? For the majority of you, you should use life insurance to replace an asset (the insured) by providing a lump-sum benefit (known as the *face amount*) to designated *beneficiaries* to replace the income lost as the result of a death. While you may consider your children to be your greatest asset, it makes no sense whatsoever to buy life insurance on them. Regardless of how important they are to you or how much you love them, they are economic liabilities, not assets.

How much life insurance do you need? In general, I'm OK with the conventional rule of thumb that coverage of twenty-five times the income to replace is appropriate.

The reason for this number follows the same logic discussed earlier regarding nest eggs. An annual withdrawal rate of 4 percent is conservative in ensuring that the income will be there for the life of the beneficiary. Multiplying the income desired by twenty-five gives you the dollar amount required to make it happen (for you math nerds out there, 4 percent is the inverse of 25). For example, if you're making $60,000 a year, you would need a life insurance policy with a death benefit of $1.5 million. Upon death, your beneficiaries can invest the proceeds in a diversified investment portfolio and have comfort in taking 4 percent annual withdrawals, or $60,000 in this example, for the remainder of their lives.

What kind of life insurance should you buy? If you want an amount of coverage anywhere close to twenty-five times your income, you can forget about *whole life* or *universal life insurance* because they are simply unaffordable. You must, in turn, opt for *term life insurance*—pure insurance that guarantees payment of a stated death benefit if the covered person dies during a specified term. The term chosen should ideally coincide with your planned retirement date or at least when your youngest child would theoretically finish college. These policies are available with a fixed *premium* (the ongoing amount paid to keep it in force) and a fixed *death benefit* providing coverage until the end of the designated term.

Statistically, the sooner you die, the longer your survivors have left to live. Another way to gauge the appropriate amount of coverage is to hypothesize the financial need should you get run over by a bus tomorrow. There are many factors to consider, and part of that discussion (which nobody wants to have) should be about how a surviving spouse or other beneficiaries should best handle the proceeds. Would you advise them to pay off the mortgage and any other outstanding debts? Should money be set aside for a college education? Is your absence going to result in a smaller household budget? Will there be new expenses, such as childcare, to take into account? There is a lot of planning to do.

The savvy life insurance salesperson will often counter this line of reasoning by highlighting the fact that, after paying all those premiums, term insurance ends up being worth nothing if you are lucky enough to live until the end

Cover Your Ass

of the term. So what? It served its purpose. If you've been following my recipe, you will have accumulated a sizable life estate by then, and the ongoing need for a death estate will no longer be an issue. The real problem here is that insurance agents don't like to sell term insurance because the commissions are paltry. Well, it's not your job to feed his family. You need to do what's in your best interest, and being "insurance poor" makes for poor planning. The affordability of term insurance provides more money for the FUEL to fund your life estate!

Harold and Maude Stevens, by the way, have two children, ages four and two. Both parents are healthy for their age, and each has a gross income of $60,000 a year. Using a multiplier of 25, they should purchase a $1.5 million term policy on each of their lives, with a minimum term of twenty years. The youngest child will be twenty-two years old by the time the coverage expires and hopefully finishing up college. A twenty-year term policy, in this case, is adequate, but when you're going through this process, be sure to compare the premium for longer-term coverage. Often the difference is small enough to warrant opting for the longer term.

- 277 -

Life insurance (death estate) works in tandem with growing your assets (life estate) by filling in the gap as you are increasing your net worth (see Table 13).

Table 13 – Harold and Maude Stevens
Life and Death Estate

Age	Life Estate ($)	Death Estate For Survivor ($)	Total ($)
35	200 000	1 500 000	1 700 000
40	378 474	1 500 000	1 878 474
45	634 966	1 500 000	2 134 966
50	998 672	1 500 000	2 498 672
55	1 509 166	1 500 000	3 009 166
60	2 219 707	0	2 219 707
65	3 202 520	0	3 202 520

A few observations to note:

♣ Without life insurance in place, the surviving spouse would have found it financially challenging to maintain the lifestyle of the remaining family members.

♣ With life insurance in place, they secure their estate if one or both of them dies prematurely.

♣ At age fifty-five, if both Harold and Maude are alive and well, they will have amassed over $3 million in their life estate—enough to produce a retirement income exceeding $10,000 a month ($4,000 a month in inflation-adjusted dollars) for the rest of their lives.

♣ It is affordable.

You can also use term life insurance to fund a tax-favored buy-sell agreement or key-person insurance policy, which can serve a useful purpose for business owners. More advanced insurance strategies can be helpful for wealthy individuals seeking to manage, grow, and preserve their wealth, but they are too sophisticated to be addressed here.

If significant health issues are present, this can cause an increase in your life insurance premium, and you may need to reduce the face amount of the policy or shorten the term to make it affordable.

♦

Do you own life insurance, and, if so, is your coverage adequate? If not, how much life insurance is right for you, and how long do you need for it to be in force?

Would your loved ones be adequately provided for if you died tomorrow?

Buy a term life insurance policy

to protect your beneficiaries

until your life estate becomes sufficient.

CHAPTER 47

PROVIDING FOR YOUR LOVED ONES

> " *A man has made at least a start on discovering the meaning of human life when he plants shade trees under which he knows full well he will never sit.*
>
> —D. Elton Trueblood

Ben Franklin remarked that the only certainties in this world are death and taxes. Have you made all the necessary preparations in the event of your death or incapacitation? Failing health or an accident may keep you from working and managing your affairs, but there's no escaping death. Do your loved ones a favor and get your ducks in a row. Stuff happens, and you should make it as easy as possible for them to sort out your affairs—just in case. It's time to do some *estate planning.*

I included this chapter in the Execution section because you must execute this task. Estate planning is an area where procrastination can prove costly. People tend to think there's no rush, preferring to handle it at a later point in time. Well, I hate to break it to you, but the timing of your death is not really up to you. There are countless examples of how the failure to implement estate planning measures had dire consequences, both financial and emotional.

Especially if you have children, start your estate planning by drafting a *will*, a document in which you specify the method for managing and distributing of your estate upon death. Talking about matters of your ultimate demise is not a particularly enjoyable experience, but that's no excuse. If your will is relatively simple, there are many inexpensive will kits available online. If your planning needs are more complicated, you'll require the services of an estate planning attorney. Regardless of the extent of your needs, take care of this matter right away.

With no will in place, the laws of the state where you are living when you die will determine the distribution of your assets. Scary thought if you ask me.

Some specifics to address in your will include:

♣ Designating a person responsible for distributing your assets. This person is called an *executor* (if male) or an *executrix* (if female). Make sure they're willing to assume the responsibility before you make it official.

♣ Choosing your beneficiaries, which could be a spouse, children, or a charity, and the percentages you want them to receive.

♣ Clarifying *guardianship*—the position of being legally responsible for the care of someone unable to care for themselves—for children who are minors should both parents die. Make sure the person you designate is willing to assume this huge responsibility.

♣ Outlining where you want your final resting place to be and how you want to spend eternity—in a coffin or an urn? Maybe you want a special song played at your funeral.

In addition to writing a will, consider drafting a *power of attorney (POA)*. This legal document allows you to designate someone, perhaps a trusted family member or attorney, to handle financial and legal matters on your behalf. The person authorized to act on your behalf is known as the *agent* or *attorney-in-fact*. The POA ends the moment you become incapacitated. A *durable power of attorney (DPOA)* is similar; however, a DPOA is valid even if you become incapacitated.

Also strongly consider a *living will,* otherwise known as an *advance directive*, that spells out your choices about life support, do-not-resuscitate orders, and any other issues that become relevant should you become incapacitated. Without a living will in place, your state has the authority to choose the person to make those end-of-life decisions for you—someone who may or may not know your wishes.

The last thing you want, in the event of your death or incapacitation, is for your spouse and children to disagree about what you would have wanted. I urge you to do your loved ones a huge favor by making your desires clear while you can. As far as costs are concerned, I have had excellent experience using Legal Zoom for many of these issues. Their full-blown estate planning packages will set you back less than $500.

Finally, create an emergency-records kit that contains everything the person you've chosen to handle your affairs would need to access. This kit should be kept in a secure location and should be shared ahead of time with a designated person. In addition to your estate-planning documents, your emergency-records kit should contain:

- ♣ Passwords
- ♣ Contact information for lawyers, bankers, investment advisers, insurance agents, etc.
- ♣ Health records
- ♣ Insurance documents
- ♣ Financial documents
- ♣ Tax returns
- ♣ Property information on homes and vehicles

Provide a copy of these documents to your executor or executrix ahead of time. If you have lost or are unable to locate any of your essential items, don't panic. You can replace them. Just don't leave that job to somebody else. Do it now. Your loved ones don't need to be rummaging through your clutter while they have a funeral to plan.

Review your estate planning documents every three to five years or when you have a life-changing event such as marriage, divorce, birth, or death to make sure the particulars are up to date. Come from a place of love and concern, and once you have a plan in place, move forward with your life knowing you've done the right thing and ensured the continued security of those you love.

◆

Do you have a will, and if so, is it up to date?

Are your relevant documents together and kept in a secure location?

Have you considered what would happen if you suddenly passed away?

Hope for the best and plan for the worst by doing your estate planning.

CHAPTER 48

ONE FOR YOU, NINETEEN FOR ME

" *The general who wins the battle makes many calcula-*
tions in his temple before the battle is fought. The gen-
eral who loses makes but few calculations beforehand.

—Sun-Tzu

George Harrison said was he was inspired to write "Tax-man" when be discovered how much he was paying in tax-es. The Beatles were earning so much money at the time that they found themselves in the top tax bracket in En-gland—approximately 95 percent. Above a certain income threshold, they kept only 5 percent of their earnings!

I don't know anyone who likes paying taxes, and April 15 might be the least favorite day of the year in the United States. Tax-sheltered investments have been around in some form or another throughout my professional life. However, it's become more difficult over the past decade for the average investor to shelter any significant money from taxation. However, there are still a handful of simple strategies that can be employed to lessen your tax burden, and you should become educated about how they can benefit you.

Tax deferral available through pre-tax retirement plans is the most common. I've already touched on this, but when you participate in one of these plans, you are essentially deferring the income on the contributions you make until they are withdrawn a later date, typically at retirement. For example, if your gross income is $60,000 a year and you're socking away $6,000 into a traditional 401(k), your taxable income for that year is reduced to $54,000. The money invested compounds tax deferred, and both the contributions and earnings are not taxed until withdrawn. Included in this mix are traditional 401(k)s, traditional IRAs, as well as similar accounts designed for self-employed individuals.

Roth 401(k)s and Roth IRAs function differently. The money invested in these retirement accounts is done on an after-tax basis and does not reduce the immediate tax bill.

The difference with after-tax retirement accounts is that the entire value of the account, including earnings, is tax-free when withdrawn (as long as specific qualifying provisions are met, such as age and particular hardships).

Choosing between these two strategies determines when the income is recognized and taxed. Either now or later, you will pay tax on that income. There are plusses and minuses for both, and it's not always a clear-cut decision as to which strategy is the most sensible to employ. What will your bracket be in retirement? Who knows? While it seems logical to presume that your income and marginal tax bracket will be lower during retirement, this likelihood is far from certain. Therefore, I suggest you hedge your bets and split the difference, to the extent possible, between both types of accounts. To use IRAs as an example, you'll want both the traditional and the Roth. When the time comes to make a withdrawal, you will have the option to pull from the IRA that makes the most sense based on the prevailing tax consequences. If your marginal income tax bracket is comparatively low, draw from the traditional IRA and pay the taxes; if it's high, tap the Roth. Diversification between pre-tax and after-tax retirement accounts provides added flexibility at retirement to lessen the tax burden.

A great option in this arena often overlooked is the *health savings account (HSA).* If you qualify for an HSA through your health insurance, you should contribute money there. Although current contribution limits are comparatively minimal, they are tax deductible. The 2020 limits are $3,550 for individuals, up to $7,100 for family coverage, plus an extra $1,000 for the over—fifty-five crowd. The withdrawals are tax-free if used for certain qualifying medical expenses, for which the list is long. Taxwise, this investment gives you the best of both worlds. If you con-tribute $5,000 to an HSA, it will reduce your taxes that year by approximately $2,000, making your out-of-pocket investment only $3,000. It is worth, however, $5,000 the minute you fund it, essentially generating an immediate, guaranteed tax-free return of $2,000 (66 percent). There's no investment I am aware of with favorable tax treatment on both the front and the back end like the HSA, and it's another bucket into which you can pour FUEL, provided you meet the requirements.

If you have money invested in the market outside of a retirement plan, you should factor the tax implications into your strategy. The beauty of using ETFs is that unlike with mutual funds, you are in control of your tax situation, and there will generally be no significant tax consequences along with way, except for income tax on dividends. The lower the taxes, the more money you will have available for growth. Profits taken down the road receive long-term capital gains treatment, which lowers the tax burden substantially.

Lastly, you should examine the tax benefits you can derive by setting up your own business, even if you are employed elsewhere. It's the last great tax shelter for the average investor. Having your own business can allow you to deduct certain expenses you may already be incurring. Anytime you can move an expense from the after-tax side to the pre-tax side of the ledger, you are reducing your tax burden. Take full advantage of the tax code; it's not just for the rich and famous.

For instance, if you like to travel for fun, consider creating a side business. I know a married couple who take three to four trips a year to exotic locales. They established an import business to purchase various products indigenous to the places they visit. After they return from their journey, they have a sale in their home. Their friends and family are always excited to see what goods they acquired, and the couple benefits from the legitimate use of the tax code. Besides deducting the cost of the trip, they earn a nice profit on the goods they sell. I would guess they travel the world for free. Works for me.

◆

Are you diversified among different types of retirement accounts?

Can you qualify for a health savings account?

What business could you establish that would provide you ancillary tax benefits?

Make the moves necessary to keep your taxes to a minimum.

CHAPTER 49

THE ANNUAL REVIEW

❝❝ *The discipline of writing something down is the first step toward making it happen.*

—Lee Iacocca

To make sure your financial plan is on track, you should schedule time with your significant other (if you're lucky enough to have one) to review the preceding year and gauge your performance. If you are operating solo, consider getting an accountability partner. Seeking accountability is not a sign of weakness. In fact, having transparency around money with another human being is nothing short of courageous.

While there are some goals you cannot control, such as investment performance, you can always focus on adhering to your budget. If you continue to allocate a minimum of 20 percent of your after-tax income to FUEL, the long-term performance should take care of itself.

Here are some questions for you to answer in writing:

- ♣ Are you still clear about where you are, where you're going, and when you want to get there?
- ♣ How well did your budget work according to the 50:30:20 budget rule?
- ♣ Is your debt on the way to being history?
- ♣ Is your emergency savings fund on the rise?
- ♣ Did you allocate a minimum of 20 percent of your after-tax income to FUEL?
- ♣ How did your investments perform?
- ♣ Are your investments appropriately diversified and consistent with your risk profile?
- ♣ Were you able to successfully divorce your emotions from your decision-making?
- ♣ Was your investing tax efficient?
- ♣ Is your life insurance adequate?
- ♣ What good habits did you acquire?
- ♣ What bad habits have you eliminated?

♣ What adjustments can you make next year to improve your financial standing?

♣ Have you given any thought to opening a side business?

♣ Most importantly, are you executing?

In addition to answering these questions, you need to quantify your performance by comparing your projected numbers with your actual results. If you have yet to do so, get comfortable with www.thecalculatorsite.com and start running financial simulations.

It's about progress, not perfection. You may want to run these calculations more frequently if it helps you maintain discipline.

◆

What other questions or calculations do you want to incorporate into your annual review?

Are you comfortable with this accountability?

Do you understand the importance of writing this stuff down?

Conduct an in-depth annual review of your performance on all fronts.

CHAPTER 50

THE MYTH OF MULTITASKING

> " *A master in the art of living draws no sharp distinction between his work and his play; his labor and his leisure; his mind and his body; his education and his recreation. He hardly knows which is which. He simply pursues his vision of excellence through whatever he is doing, and leaves others to determine whether he is working or playing. To himself, he always appears to be doing both.*
>
> —Lawrence Pearsall Jacks

In today's technological world, the distractions are myriad. Being present these days is a massive undertaking, yet it is so vital to living a full, productive, happy life. It takes effort. While technology has enhanced many facets of our lives, it has, in many ways, done just the opposite by making life more complicated—a classic double-edged sword.

Google provides unlimited access to information with a simple keystroke. The internet is so fraught with fake news that it's hard to know what to believe anymore. Chiropractic and orthopedic care practitioners have a lucrative future in the offing, given the inevitable back problems of a generation continuously hunched over their smartphones. Self-driving cars may be the solution to the recklessness of texting while driving. My parents think I'm a technological wiz, and my children poke fun at me for being technologically disadvantaged. The times, they are a-changing. While it's mind-blowing to this baby boomer how I can make a video call to the other side of the planet at no cost, I'm not fond of the expectations of twenty-four-seven availability at the touch of somebody's button.

As a recovered alcoholic, I am hardwired for addictive behavior, and those propensities don't appear to be subsiding anytime soon. They are embedded in my DNA. This behavior can show up in so many areas, be it work, leisure, reading, writing, food, women, or poker. Visual and audio stimuli are ubiquitous, and it takes a ton of discipline on my part to resist being yanked one way and then another.

Although I prefer reading over watching TV, I'm not above getting caught up in a Netflix binge now and then like everyone else. All too often, a simple Google search leads to my venturing down endless rabbit holes for hours reading stuff that is a colossal waste of time.

How can you make life simpler and more balanced? Begin by accepting the fact that multitasking is a myth. In reality, the human mind can only focus on one thing at a time, and any attempt to do otherwise translates into mediocre performance across the board. Buddhists have a name for the mental state of being unsettled, restless, or confused: *monkey mind.* I was a reasonably competitive golfer in a previous life, when I was a seventeen-year-old with no real job, no spouse, no mortgage, and no current events that concerned me to any significant extent. When I was swinging the golf club, it had my full and undivided focus. As I got older and the distractions increased, the monkey mind gradually took over my golf game, a sad and pathetic consequence of bringing mental clutter with me every time I play.

The only way I have learned to calm down the monkey mind is to meditate, which I now do daily. I need to shut my brain down every so often to pursue peacefulness and some degree of clarity. I have become increasingly aware of the times when my mind begins to run amok, and meditating works well in restoring me to relative sanity.

One of the reasons I am a good poker player is that the game captures my full and undivided attention. It's a meditation unto itself, much like working on a jigsaw puzzle while listening to the sound of rain hitting the roof. If only I could do the same with my golf game. I guess there's always tomorrow.

You can become more balanced by striving to be more present in a world where everything around you is clamoring for attention. We all need time for work and time for play. Time to read and time to play with the kids. Time to do nothing. The old nine-to-five paradigm is rapidly becoming a relic of the past.

The days of leaving work behind at the office are slowly giving way to a new era of flextime and remote work options, creating a formidable challenge to keep your work life from bleeding into your personal life.

How do you keep this line from becoming increasingly blurred? How do you adapt to the new normal? Are you cool with your teenager plopping down their phone on the dinner table? Is it too much to ask someone to turn off the TV when you're in the middle of a conversation? What's the deal with all these people running around with pasta hanging out of their ears?

♦

Is your life truly balanced?

Do you embrace technology, or does it embrace you?

When was the last time you sat still and quietly pondered?

Give up all attempts to multitask, and strive to be present to the task at hand.

CHAPTER 51

EXECUTION RECAP

" *The difference between what we do and what we are capable of doing would suffice to solve most of the world's problems.*

—Mahatma Gandhi

This book contains the tools you need to get you from where you are to where you want to be. I have strived to make a seemingly complicated process as simple as possible, such that anyone can do it. But you have to be the one to do it. Execution is where the rubber meets the road.

- ♣ Be coachable and follow the recipe.
- ♣ Quantify your end game and keep that target in your sights.
- ♣ Assess and quantify your current financial condition.
- ♣ Make the 50:30:20 budget rule a part of your life.

- ♣ Ration your FUEL to eliminate debt, add to your emergency savings fund, and invest.

- ♣ Design the plan to get you from Point A to Point B.

- ♣ The road to financial success is a grind, and time is your ally.

- ♣ Decide where you want to invest with a preference toward tax-deferred accounts.

- ♣ Follow the guidelines for how to invest, making substitutions where necessary.

- ♣ Build an investment portfolio of passive ETFs consistent with your time horizon.

- ♣ Become a DIY investor and pocket the difference.

- ♣ Protect your family in the event of your demise by purchasing affordable term life insurance.

- ♣ Take care of your estate planning needs immediately.

- ♣ Be tax savvy.

- ♣ Review your financials in detail annually, charting your course and making the necessary adjustments.

- ♣ Develop an increased sense of being present.

Create your plan

and follow it to its natural conclusion.

CHAPTER 52

WAXING PHILOSOPHICAL

 What is not started today is never finished tomorrow.

—Johann Wolfgang von Goethe

Beginning with my first visit to Las Vegas in the summer of 1978, the casino environment, particularly the poker table, has been my laboratory for contemplating the human condition and its relationship to money. Some players win, many more lose, and the house takes its piece regardless.

Why do people continue to play games and make bad bets with the odds stacked so squarely against them? Why don't people take the time to study the games before they put their hard-earned money at risk? Why does every poker player I know think they're better than average?

It's no different when it comes to the world of investing and personal money management. Why do so few people retire with financial dignity in a country where op-portunities for wealth creation abound? Why do people make investments in things they don't understand? How is it that money sticks to some and not to others? Why is in-come inequality so pervasive? These are just a few examples of the endless questions that give me pause and compelled me to write this book.

I am the product of trial and error, having made more mistakes than I can chronicle in this book. Procrastination kept this book from being finished earlier. A lot earlier. Even though I had acquired the requisite knowledge years earlier, the lessons I've shared with you in this book weren't practiced by me at all until much later in life. Big hat, no cattle. All talk, no action. I am painstakingly aware of the chasm that exists between knowledge and execution, but those days are history.

Likewise, you must commit to bridge that gap.

Although I have been in the money-management world my entire adult life, the twisted irony is that I don't care that much about money—at least not in the manner most people do. I understand that we need it. It facilitates the exchange of goods and services. My youngest daughter is a brilliant musician who laments the fact that she has to grapple with the concept of time. She contends that the world would be a better place without it and would prefer to live totally in the present with no distinctions called past or future. I likewise bemoan the necessity of money. What would the world look like if there was no such thing as money? I have witnessed up close the downside of what money and greed can do, and there was a time in my life when I didn't want any part of it.

On the other hand, I have seen the enormous good that money can do. I have needs and wants just like everybody else. I had to find a way to embrace the attributes of wealth without allowing money to exert the power over me it once enjoyed.

In time, I began to treat the flow of money in and out of my life as a game, and it became necessary for me to become adept at playing the game well. Slowly but surely, I figured it out and finally got good at it. To be able to share what I have learned by writing this book has been tremendously gratifying.

There's a friendly neighborhood poker game I play in where a twenty-dollar win is a big night. Playing gin rummy with my mom is likely to result in losses (usually mine) that can approach a whole dollar! (There are, however, significant bragging rights that are hard to put a price on.) The truth is I love all these endeavors equally. A game is a game.

In both poker and financial planning, money per se is no longer the motivating factor for me. It just so happens that money often comes as the result of learning to play the game well. Adopting that perspective has made the game more enjoyable for me to play.

No matter how many mistakes you have made in the past, you can turn your boat around. Don't sell yourself short; much of this you can do yourself. Compound interest is indeed the eighth wonder of the world. Building wealth is just another game, and in this book, I have provided you with strategies for playing. Roll up your sleeves and get busy!

Keep it simple, maintain perspective, and enjoy the ride.

Shuffle up and deal.

If you can keep your head when all about you

Are losing theirs and blaming it on you;

If you can trust yourself when all men doubt you,

But make allowance for their doubting too:

If you can wait and not be tired by waiting,

Or, being lied about, don't deal in lies,

Or being hated don't give way to hating,

And yet don't look too good, nor talk too wise;

If you can dream — and not make dreams your master;

If you can think — and not make thoughts your aim,

If you can meet with Triumph and Disaster

And treat those two impostors just the same;

If you can bear to hear the truth you've spoken

Twisted by knaves to make a trap for fools,

Or watch the things you gave your life to, broken,

And stoop and build 'em up with worn-out tools;

If you can make one heap of all your winnings

And risk it on one turn of pitch-and-toss,

And lose, and start again at your beginnings,

And never breathe a word about your loss:

If you can force your heart and nerve and sinew

To serve your turn long after they are gone,

And so hold on when there is nothing in you

Except the Will which says to them: "Hold on!"

If you can talk with crowds and keep your virtue,

Or walk with Kings—nor lose the common touch,

If neither foes nor loving friends can hurt you,

If all men count with you, but none too much:

If you can fill the unforgiving minute

With sixty seconds' worth of distance run,

Yours is the Earth and everything that's in it,

And— which is more— you'll be a Man, my son!

From "If" by Rudyard Kipling

ACKNOWLEDGMENTS

Writing this book was immensely gratifying but did not come without its challenges. I could not have done it without the support, encouragement, and love of so many.

To my editors, Janet Wagner and Jesse Winter, for believing that what I had to say was relevant. You convinced me that the world needed to hear what I wanted to share. Thank you for your patience and for encouraging me to become a real writer.

To Doug Dalton, former director of poker operations at Bellagio Las Vegas, for his generosity and kindness in introducing me to his friends in the world of high-stakes poker. Your enthusiasm for my book idea gave me the early encouragement to move forward.

To Lyle Berman, businessman extraordinaire, multiple—World Series of Poker bracelet winner, and member of the Poker Hall of Fame, for taking the time to entertain me with his countless poker stories. You understood and appreciated the dots I was trying to connect.

To the late Chip Reese, arguably the best poker player who ever lived, who took time to teach a novice like me how to play poker. Rest in peace.

To Tim Ferris, for opening my eyes to a better lifestyle.

To my buds at my local poker game—Farley, Deano, Johnny G, Smitty, and Booker—thank you for making me laugh and helping me pay the rent.

To Deborah Price, author, and founder of the Money Coaching Institute, for your invaluable insight into behavioral money coaching.

To my former investment clients for trusting that I would always put their interests ahead of mine. It was a pleasure to have been your financial adviser.

To those of you in recovery, thanks for being there for me. Keep fighting the good fight.

Lastly, thanks to all the people who have shared their stories and expertise with me over the years.

Made in the USA
Columbia, SC
27 April 2021